East Asian Popular Culture

Series Editors

Yasue Kuwahara, Department of Communication, Northern Kentucky University, Highland Heights, KY, USA
John A. Lent, International Journal of Comic Art, Drexel Hill, PA, USA

This series focuses on the study of popular culture in East Asia (referring to China, Hong Kong, Japan, Mongolia, North Korea, South Korea, and Taiwan) in order to meet a growing interest in the subject among students as well as scholars of various disciplines. The series examines cultural production in East Asian countries, both individually and collectively, as its popularity extends beyond the region. It continues the scholarly discourse on the recent prominence of East Asian popular culture as well as the give and take between Eastern and Western cultures.

More information about this series at
https://link.springer.com/bookseries/14958

Kyong Yoon

Diasporic Hallyu

The Korean Wave in Korean Canadian Youth Culture

Kyong Yoon
Department of English
and Cultural Studies
University of British Columbia
Okanagan
Kelowna, BC, Canada

ISSN 2634-5935 ISSN 2634-5943 (electronic)
East Asian Popular Culture
ISBN 978-3-030-94966-2 ISBN 978-3-030-94964-8 (eBook)
https://doi.org/10.1007/978-3-030-94964-8

Cover credit: AsiaVision/Getty Images

This Palgrave Macmillan imprint is published by the registered company Springer Nature Switzerland AG
The registered company address is: Gewerbestrasse 11, 6330 Cham, Switzerland

PREFACE

As of 2021, transnational Korean media is circulated globally far beyond Korean ethnic communities and the trend is more than a fad. As evidenced by enthusiastic K-pop fandom comprised of young people of various cultural backgrounds and nationalities, the Korean Wave (or Hallyu) phenomenon has global cultural significance. In highlighting the experiences of the global and diverse populations of Hallyu audiences, this book focuses on diasporic Korean youth whose engagement with Hallyu media might be different from older ethnic Korean populations and other global audiences.

This project began with the aim of understanding Korean Canadian youth and their engagement with the transnational phenomenon of Hallyu. As a first generation Korean immigrant researcher in Canada, I have been curious to explore how young Korean Canadians—especially children of immigrants who have grown up on the margins of the White dominant cultural frame—negotiate their cultural identity through Hallyu media (K-pop and Korean TV in particular) that originated in their ancestral homeland, yet has emerged globally. The analysis reveals that the diasporic youth's identity work takes place in between different cultural contexts and in between different media texts. Drawing on in-depth interviews with young people of diasporic backgrounds (1.5 generation and second generation Korean Canadians in their teens and twenties), this book develops the framework of the *diasporic dimensions* of Hallyu, revealing that Hallyu is far more than outbound flows of made-in-Korea cultural content. For young Korean Canadians, Hallyu media is signified not only as an ethnic media form but also as a global media practice through which they can make sense of who they are without necessarily relying on the White dominant cultural frame or an essentialized mode of ethnicity. As proposed in this book, the diasporic dimensions of Hallyu reveal that Hallyu may potentially be counter-hegemonic against dominant structural forces that define the transnational Korean cultural wave from either a Western-centric or a nation-statist perspective.

Given that there are a limited number of studies of diasporic Korean youth or the Korean Wave in Canadian contexts, it is hoped that this book can be a milestone in Korean Canadian youth studies and Hallyu research. By using a diasporic lens to explore the hybrid and dynamic cultural processes of the Korean Wave, the book offers an alternative framework to supplement and contribute to the existing analyses of transnational audiences of the Hallyu phenomenon.

While writing this book, I have learned substantially from the life experiences and stories of the diasporic young people. I have also learned there are far more diasporic youth stories to be told and shared in the time of the Korean Wave. Hoping to conduct a follow-up project to explore further the diasporic dimensions of Hallyu, I would like to thank all the people who contributed to this book, including the following:

First of all, I respectfully acknowledge the Syilx Okanagan Nation and their peoples, in whose traditional, ancestral, unceded territory I live.

Second, I am grateful to Professor Dal Yong Jin at Simon Fraser University, who has encouraged me to look forward and experiment with new ideas for this book and other projects. He has been a great inspiration for my academic journey for over a decade, and I feel that I cannot thank him enough as I have learned so much from his exceptional scholarship and insights.

Third, I would like to thank my colleagues at the University of British Columbia (Okanagan and Vancouver) and elsewhere for their collegial support—especially, Dr. Dan Keyes, Dr. David Jefferess, Dr. Ruthann Lee, Dr. Maria Alexopoulos, Dr. Karis Shearer, Dr. Shirley Chau, Dr. Hyung-Gu Lynn, Professor Ross King, Professor Don Baker, Dr. Alifa Bandali, Dr. Kyoungrok Ko, Dr. Wonjung Min, Professor Sun Sun Lim, Professor Hilary Pilkington, Amanda Brobbel, and Lori Walter. I also appreciate the Faculty of Creative and Critical Studies' generous support of the 2020 Faculty Fellowship, with which I was able to focus on writing this book. This open access publication was supported by the UBC Open Access Fund for Humanities and Social Sciences and the UBC FCCS Research Support Fund.

Fourth, I am indebted to several exceptional research assistants over the past six years. It was an absolute pleasure to work with the Korean Canadian assistants YounJeen Kim, Jina Ko, Song Yi Jeon, and NuRee Lee, who provided invaluable support for the field studies.

Last but not least, this book is my humble dedication to young Korean Canadians—including the interview participants.

Kelowna, Canada   Kyong Yoon
September 2021

Note to Readers

In this book, Korea refers to the Republic of Korea (South Korea) unless otherwise stated. In Romanization of Korean sources and names, the Revised Romanization of Korean is used except for already established customs such as a person's name and locations. All interview participant names presented in this book are pseudonyms.

CONTENTS

CHAPTER 1

Introduction: Thinking the Korean Wave Diasporically

Abstract Despite increasing scholarly and media attention to the global circulation of Korean media and popular culture (the Korean Wave or Hallyu), the diasporic population has remained a grey area in the literature. As early adopters and cultural translators, diasporic Korean youth have played a pivotal role in the recent rise of the Korean Wave. Furthermore, this cultural wave can be considered metaphorically diasporic as it contributes to the exposure of global audiences to the mediated experiences of migration and hybridity, whereby the boundaries of the nation-state are questioned. As diaspora is a way of imagining borders, groups, and individuals that deal with cultural difference, the conceptual lens of diaspora can advance audience studies of Hallyu.

Keywords The Korean Wave (Hallyu) · Diasporic Hallyu · Diasporic youth · Hallyu in Canada · Diaspora · Soft power

The Korean Wave (or Hallyu), which refers to the global circulation of Korean media and popular culture, seems more visible than ever, despite almost two decades of doubt, skepticism, and disapproval about its continuation. In particular, the rapid surge of K-pop (Korean idol pop music) in the global mediascape, led by several idol groups and their dedicated overseas fans since the mid-2010s, reveals an unprecedented media phenomenon spotlighting a non-Western, once-peripheral

K. Yoon, *Diasporic Hallyu*, East Asian Popular Culture,
https://doi.org/10.1007/978-3-030-94964-8_1

cultural location and signaling a challenge to the Western-centric medi-ascape. This continued rise of Hallyu was not particularly predicted even among its longtime, overseas fans. Indeed, some of this book's early inter-view participants were not certain about the continuation of Korean pop culture recognition in North America. In a 2015 interview, 25-year-old interviewee Luke in Toronto ascribed the Korean Wave to the enhanced accessibility of digital media (including illegal streaming sites) and thus described it as an exaggeration.

> The Korean Wave that people in Korea try to understand is a bit over-exaggerated. Because of globalization, people are more acquainted with other cultures and fanatic about Korean stuff. So, yes, people are more exposed to Korean cultures, norms, and food, and of course K-pop. But, is that because Korean culture is suddenly more competitive and superior to other cultures and media? I don't think so. I think it's more of, because of the Internet, for example, YouTube.

Luke considered the Korean Wave as an Internet-driven fad that may disappear or be replaced with another fad sooner or later. While more interviewees were relatively optimistic about the continued rise of Hallyu in Canada, there were still a few interview participants like Luke who were uncertain. At least until the mid-2010s, the world seemed skeptical about (if not indifferent to) the destiny of the Korean Wave. In an interna-tional survey conducted by a Korean government-sponsored organization in 2012, over 60% of the survey respondents predicted that the Korean Wave would fade out within 4 years (Korea Foundation for International Cultural Exchange 2012).[1]

In stark contrast to this gloomy forecast, the Korean Wave has survived for a decade since the survey. Several months after the survey, Psy's

---

[1] Interestingly, this survey revealed that even Asian respondents were not necessarily more optimistic than Western respondents about the future of the Wave. These results may be explained partly by the emerging anti-Korean Wave sentiments in several Asian countries that had led the early boom of Korean drama and music since the late 1990s (Ahn and Yoon 2020; H. Lee 2017; Sakamoto and Allen 2007). For example, Japan is known for its large number of consumers of Korean music and drama but is also known for rigorous anti-Korea and anti-Korean Wave campaigns (H. Lee 2017). This tendency illustrates that, due to historical tensions (e.g., colonial memories between Korea and Japan), intra-Asian cultural flows such as the Korean Wave have often encountered backlashes, while generating favorable audiences drawing on cultural proximities.

"Gangnam Style" smashed the global mediascape, whereas many K-pop songs, Korean dramas (known as K-drama), and Korean films have increasingly been circulated beyond Korean or Asian borders throughout the 2010s. The Korean Wave has continued through the 2010s and now the 2020s. Its scope is not local or regional but certainly global. The continued wave has been supported by the Korean government's initiatives and investments in cultural industries (Jin 2016 and 2018), and thus, Hallyu has been branded as "soft power" of Korea—referring to the attractive power of the country's culture (Nye and Kim 2013). More importantly, technology-equipped fans have led the Wave as a cultural trend of grassroots transnationalism. Digital technology has not only increased the global availability of and access to Korean cultural texts but also allowed global audiences to translate and participate in the transcultural flows (Jin et al. 2021; S. Y. Kim 2018).

The global circulation of cultural products from a non-Western country may not be unique to the Korean Wave as there have been other examples for decades. However, prior to the Korean Wave, those examples tended to fade out after a short term of success or circulate primarily intra-regionally (e.g., Hong Kong films); otherwise, those examples tended to be represented by a specific genre (e.g., Japanese anime), rather than involving multiple and transmedia genres. In comparison, the Korean Wave may include a wider range of genres and texts (Jin et al. 2021). K-pop, K-drama, and other media genres have synergistically attracted overseas fan audiences through transmedia storytelling accelerated by digital media convergence.

The Korean Wave phenomenon suggests new questions about the processes, directions, effects, and meanings of transnational cultural flows. Above all, while transnational cultural flows have until recently been observed and analyzed in terms of the diffusion of the (Western) center and norms, the Korean Wave reveals alternative routes in transnational cultural circulation. Moreover, from a political economy perspective, the Wave questions how local cultural content and industries expand to be integrated into global cultural markets and mediascape (Jin 2016). Furthermore, from an audience studies perspective, Hallyu also proposes the question of how transnational and transcultural affinities between the overseas audiences and Korean cultural content emerge (Han 2017).

Like other transnational cultural phenomena, the Korean Wave phenomenon may have emerged and evolved through complicated

processes rather than having a clear cut, lineal history. Despite the complicated ebbs and flows of transnational Korean media and popular culture,
scholarly and media discourses have attempted to identify the origin and
history of Hallyu in a linear, evolutional narrative. For example, the Wave
is defined in different, yet lineal phases, such as Hallyu 1.0 (the period
during which Korean media was extensively diffused in Asia) and Hallyu
2.0 (the period during which Korean media circulates not only in Asia
but also in non-Asian locations especially via social and digital media)
(Jin et al. 2021; Lee and Nornes 2015). The linear discourse of the
Korean Wave has often traced the origin of this cultural trend by examining the terminology of the Korean Wave or Hallyu. The term Korean
Wave, which was first popularized by Asian news media and then by the
Korean cultural industries and government, has been used widely since
the late 1990s—first in Asia and then globally (Yoon and Kang 2017).
As implied in its name, the Korean Wave has been perceived as ebbs and
flows with a clear national origin—Korea.

Despite debates about the nature and histories of Hallyu, it is undeniable that the Korean Wave has captured continued global media attention,
and Korean media products have been popular especially among young
people (Jin et al. 2021). After its initial popularity among groups of young
people via social media and online media, Hallyu has increasingly been
integrated into mainstream media platforms. Especially in the US, K-pop
and K-dramas have frequently been reported on through influential news
media outlets, including *The New York Times* and *Forbes*. Undeniably,
some made-in-Korea pop culture items have obtained remarkable cultural
recognition, especially since the 2010s. If Psy's "Gangnam Style" was
an unexpected, viral phenomenon, a newer cultural wave represented by
such names as BTS, Blackpink, *Parasite* (film), *Kingdom* (Netflix original series), and *The Masked Singer* (TV show franchise) has revealed the
possibility of sustainable growth for Hallyu. Owing to the growth of its
audience bases and mainstream media coverage, Korean popular culture
has been integrated into the global mediascape. Many overseas audiences
are familiar with such terms as K-pop, K-drama, *meokbang* (or spelled
as *mukbang*; livestreamed eating shows), and other Korean pop culture
terminologies. Seoul has earned the reputation of a global pop culture
hub (Y. Oh 2018).

To capture and analyze the important transnational moments of
Hallyu, an increasing number of monographs and anthologies have been
published (e.g., Choi and Maliangkay 2015; Chua and Iwabuchi 2008;

Jin 2016; Jin et al. 2021; G. Kim 2018; S. Y. Kim 2018; Y. Kim 2013; Kuwahara 2014; Lee and Nornes 2015). In particular, audience studies have increasingly examined how cultural differences are translated and cultural affinities are explored between K-pop and its fans who are linguistically and culturally distant from K-pop (Jin et al. 2021). As Jenkins et al. (2013) have suggested, transnational media flows tend to be facilitated by either (a) "diasporas" (or "immigrants") who disseminate media of their origin (homelands or ancestral homelands) in the country of resettlement and operate as proselytizers or (b) "cosmopolitans" who consume media produced outside of their own geocultural contexts.[2] Whereas the literature on the Korean Wave has paid increasing attention to the "cosmopolitan" audiences (e.g., overseas fans of K-pop), particular groups of overseas fans—such as diasporic audiences—remain relatively under-researched.

To address a gap in studies about the Korean Wave, this book explores a research area that has insufficiently been examined—the diasporic dimensions of the Korean Wave. It claims that Hallyu is diasporic in interwoven ways. First, Hallyu explicitly involves diasporic cultural flows. Korean migrants and their cultural experiences are deeply integrated into the ongoing circulation of this cultural wave. In particular, diasporic Korean youth engage with, and contribute to, the emergence of Hallyu through their bicultural literacy and in-between-ness. Second, Hallyu is metaphorically diasporic in that this cultural wave reveals that not only Korean migrants but also other global media audiences are becoming diasporic through mediated and embodied experiences. Hallyu may remind us that, in a broad sense, "we are all migrants" (Feldman 2015), as the foreign cultural content might lead its audiences to question their own sense of belonging to the nation-state they inhabit. Among

---

[2] While Jenkins et al.'s (2013) categorization may present useful ideal types for understanding transnational media flows and audiences, the naming of and binary oppositions between "cosmopolitans" and "immigrants" seem problematic. In this binary model, "cosmopolitans" are signified relatively positively (implying more forward looking) compared to "diasporas/immigrants" who seem to be signified as backward looking and attached to their ancestral past. However, in reality, the "cosmopolitans" may include settler residents who are interested in foreign media only through niche foreign media and have very limited transnational mobilities. Moreover, realities are not captured by this binary framework because, for example, children of immigrants are equipped with highly multicultural literacy and thus have many opportunities to access different cultures, even compared to conventional "cosmopolitans" (e.g., White Canadians who are born and raised in Canada).

these two diasporic dimensions, this book focuses on the former—diasporic Korean audiences' engagement with Hallyu—throughout its empirical chapters (Chapters 2–4), while the latter—metaphorical diasporas among Hallyu audiences—will be addressed as a future research agenda, especially in this first chapter and the concluding chapter.

Hallyu Through a Diasporic Lens

This book examines an under-researched audience group—diasporic youth—in the process of Hallyu. Diaspora in this book refers to people of migrant backgrounds (1.5 or second generation, as discussed later in this chapter). In doing so, a particular area of transnational popular cultural flows—the diasporic dimensions of pop cultural flows—will be explored. Despite ongoing debates about its definition, the concept of diaspora is considered to offer several advantages (compared to other similar concepts such as immigration). Most of all, diaspora "provides an alternative to a nation-statist understanding of immigration and assimilation" (Brubaker 2005, p. 13). Transnational ties and new social formations facilitated by diaspora challenge the boundaries of the nation. Diaspora as a scattered group of people and culture can engage with "both syncretic cultural formation and re-enforced ethnic and nationalist ties" (Kalra et al. 2005, p. 33). For example, diasporic Koreans may have their long-distance nationalism (Anderson 1998) through which they seek ties with their (ancestral) homeland or may develop a sense of belonging to the nation-state in which they currently reside. However, diaspora may not necessarily seek identity of either/or but rather explore a new sense of belonging. Diaspora can create "new identities which have no affiliation to the nation-state form" (Kalra et al. 2005, p. 33). As Brah (1996, p. 194) suggested, the concept of diaspora questions the discourse of fixed origins while giving attention to "a homing desire"—realized through "feeling at home" in multi-places rather than "declaring a place as home." In so doing, diaspora allows us to think through borders and reflexively engage with cultural differences. Diaspora is a way of imagining borders, groups, and individuals "dealing with cultural difference on a daily basis, in the communities where they live and work, intermarrying, mixing cultures and races, growing up bilingual and trilingual and resisting (or succumbing to) pressures to become (or to pretend to become) monolingual" (Robinson 1997, p. 29).

Diaspora and Hallyu

Given the conceptual merits of diaspora, a close examination of diasporic Korean audiences' engagement with Hallyu may contribute to moving beyond the nation-statist understanding of Hallyu (as an export of Korea and its penetration into imagined global markets). However, despite flourishing interest in Hallyu, existing studies have not articulated diaspora as a research area. Media and cultural studies have increasingly produced academic publications on Hallyu—from political economy analysis of the Korean government's policies behind Hallyu (e.g., Jin 2018) to ethnographic analysis of overseas K-pop fans (e.g., S. Y. Kim 2018). However, the flourishing analyses of this phenomenon appear to focus primarily on the "K" component of this phenomenon—whether in a celebratory or critical tone. That is, scholars seem to be intrigued by the global diffusion of cultural products made in Korea—a country that used to be in a marginal or peripheral status in global cultural industries. The rise of this cultural trend originating in a non-Western context and diffused across a wide range of different locations has attracted academic attention and has been analyzed as an example of cultural heterogenization or cultural hybridization (Jin 2016; Ryoo 2009). The existing research (especially English language literature) has largely addressed the ways in which Hallyu is intensified and widespread by examining government policies, industries' strategies, and audience reception. More specifically, audience studies of Hallyu have addressed overseas fans of K-pop or K-drama. An increasing number of studies of K-pop fans have been published along with the exceptional popularity of a few K-pop artists, such as BTS, and thus have contributed to fandom studies. Such contributions are noteworthy, given that transnational fandom studies are still nascent (Chin and Morimoto 2013; Han 2017).

The existing audience studies of Hallyu and their focus on overseas fans of Korean media and pop culture tend to pay limited attention to diasporas, while focusing on particularly dedicated audience members such as overseas fans who do not have any diasporic ties to Korea—or "pop cosmopolitans" to use Jenkins et al.'s (2013) term. Overall, overseas young people of ethnic Korean backgrounds have been relatively under-researched, with a few exceptions (D. C. Oh 2015; J. S. Park 2013). Perhaps diasporic Koreans may have been taken for granted in studies of Hallyu, as they are familiar with the language and culture and have already been consuming Korean media through their transnational connections and in ethnic communities even before the emergence of Hallyu. However, diasporic youth of Korean backgrounds who have some familiarity with Korean culture and language do not inherently identify with Hallyu. Their engagement with the Hallyu media often involves complicated processes and identifications. For example, the Korean Canadian diasporic youth discussed in this book do not explicitly belong to the Korean mediascape, while being marginally situated in the Canadian mediascape. They navigate different media environments across different languages and cultures. Depending on their familiarity with Korean cultural heritage, diasporic youth have to translate and relocalize Hallyu media from their own socio-cultural positions.

The diasporic youth's engagement with Hallyu reveals how popular cultural forms flow beyond cultural boundaries of nationality or ethnicity. However, diasporic youth are not entirely free of the nationalizing or ethnicizing forces inscribed in Hallyu media and discourse (Koh and Baek 2020). The top-down discourse of Hallyu often engages with the rhetoric of "soft power" that associates this cultural trend with national pride and power in competition with other countries (Walsh 2014). Despite the nationalistic discourse of Hallyu, Korean media and popular culture have rapidly been hybridized in form and content. As clearly shown in the K-pop genre, the Hallyu industries and creators have rigorously experimented with different formats, styles, and narratives. In particular, the cultural wave of Hallyu has extensively deployed digital media technologies as well as human talents (e.g., K-pop idols) (Liew 2021) through its unique "in-house systems" where global talents collaborate under the umbrella of K-brands (e.g., K-pop). For example, K-pop has incorporated foreign languages (English in particular) and invited foreign talents into its production processes to a large extent, while thus refusing to be pigeonholed as a set of cultural products from Korea.

Diasporic Youth in Hallyu

Due to their cultural and linguistic literacy, diasporic Korean youth have played a pivotal role in the recent rise of Hallyu as early adopters, "proselytizers," and/or cultural brokers. In particular, it is probable that some diasporic audience members, partly due to their cultural knowledge and early adopter position, play a role as proselytizers in spreading their ethnic culture transnationally (Jenkins et al. 2013). Diasporic Korean youth have contributed to the production of paratexts (e.g., fan-created subtitles) and construction of overseas Hallyu infrastructure (e.g., venture companies specializing in K-drama streaming services) (Hu 2010; J. S. Park 2013). For example, as further discussed in Chapter 3, the popular K-drama streaming site Viki was co-founded by three young entrepreneurs, two of whom are Korean Americans, and diasporic Korean audiences have also generated content (such as translations) in the global circulation of K-dramas. Diasporic young people may serve as cultural translators (i.e., those who offer linguistic translation and/or offer cultural knowledge in various online audience forums) and thus potentially play a role in brokering or gatekeeping the overseas content in the Canadian medias-cape. K. Yoon (2020) defined diasporic Korean youth as linguistic and cultural translators, as they contributed to the rise of Hallyu through their participation in digital media-driven translation processes. He claimed that diasporic youth "translate Hallyu literally by producing subtitles for a larger audience and re-localize Korean media culturally in a transnational context" (p. 153).

Diasporic Korean youth are not simply early adopters and consumers but also contribute to the production of Hallyu media. For example, an increasing number of overseas youth of Korean backgrounds have participated in K-pop industries. In particular, the involvement of young Korean Canadians and Korean Americans in the K-pop scenes has rein-forced trans-Pacific connections and genre hybridizations by introducing American pop music and hip-hop to K-pop industries and vice versa (J. S. Park 2013). Addressing North American youth culture, J. S. Park (2013) argued that Korean Americans have left a footprint in Korean popular culture, claiming that they are among the key creators of transnational Hallyu. The diasporic audiences' contributions to and engagement with Hallyu may reveal how cultures are recontextualized and hybridized. The diasporic dimensions of Hallyu remind us that transnational Korean media is a highly hybrid cultural form (Jin 2016), and its diasporic audiences are hyphenated, hybrid subjects who negotiate different mediascapes.

A diasporic lens is not simply to magnify the romanticized notion of hybridity and difference. Rather, studies of diasporic audiences may offer an antidote to celebratory discourses about the frequent genre/style mixes that are observed in recent Korean media. Hallyu industries' exten-sive style blending has been criticized for their highly commodified production systems and lack of counter-hegemonic forces—what Bhabha

(1994) called "the third space" (Jin 2016; G. Kim 2018). The celebratory discourse of hybridity may conceal existing power relations, such as gender/race relations, while removing the contexts and histories behind the hybridization of different cultural forms. Critics argue that the inflated discourse of (postmodern) hybridity may serve to flatten the social issues of injustice and power hierarchies and to interpellate us as consumers in global capitalism (García Canclini 2000). In this regard, the diasporic lens offers an antidote to both the nation-statist understanding of culture and the post-national (and de-politicized) imagination of hybrid cultures.

As examined throughout this book, Korean Canadian youth's understanding of and participation in the transnational wave of Korean popular culture are different from those of native Korean youth on the one hand and those of Canadian youth of various backgrounds (i.e., non-Korean backgrounds) on the other hand. By closely engaging with young Korean Canadians, this book addresses an under-researched and underrepresented group of audiences of transnational Korean media and popular culture—diasporic youth as a significant audience group in understanding and exploring the transnational meanings of Hallyu.

STUDYING DIASPORIC YOUTH

Despite increasing transnational mobilities, diasporic youth have attracted relatively limited academic attention. They are situated to negotiate different cultural identities. They are subject to multiple modes of belonging and thus carry "hyphenated identity" (Colombo 2014; Kalra et al. 2005). Their bilingual and bicultural capacities may allow them to appropriate different cultural resources more easily than their peers of the dominant ethno-racial group (e.g., White people in North American contexts). However, multiple cultural belonging may also involve uncertainty in self-identification (Colombo and Rebughini 2012). In this respect, it is increasingly important to understand how diasporic youth access different media and explore their sense of belonging in the process of global migration and mobility. In particular, diasporic young people engage with media from their *ancestral* homeland in relation to the media of their *current* homeland. Given that different media may offer different means of identity work and identification, diasporic young people whose sense of belonging is multifaceted may negotiate their bicultural or multicultural affiliations through various media. As Gigi Durham (2004, p. 140) aptly pointed out, young people's "struggles with identity can be compared with the identity questions experienced by transnational immigrants: in the liminal spaces between childhood and adulthood, or between one geopolitical state and another, the 'Who am I?' question becomes imperative." However, the literature has insufficiently addressed how diasporic youth engage with different media forms and content in the process of renegotiating their identities.

This book focuses on Korean Canadian youth in relation to their engagement with transnational Korean media and popular culture. While Korean Canadian youth can refer to a wide range of young people of Korean cultural backgrounds living in Canada, this book will focus on 1.5 and second generation youth—those who were born in Korea and migrated to Canada during their childhood (i.e., 1.5 generation, or 1.5-ers) and those who were born into Korean immigrant families and raised in Canada (i.e., second generation). According to the sociological literature, the 1.5 generation refers to foreign-born people who immigrated before the age of 12–13 (before entrance to secondary schools) and are children of first generation immigrants (Danico 2004; Rumbaut 2012). Of course, even within the 1.5 generation category, diasporic young peoples' experiences may vary depending on when their migration occurred (e.g., early childhood, middle childhood, or adolescence); thus, 1.5 generation could mean more specifically those who arrive in the "host" country at the ages of 6–12 and thus are relatively likely to "adapt flexibly between two worlds and to become fluent bilinguals" (Rumbaut 2012, p. 983). The second generation—those who were born and raised in Canada—also have diverse experiences especially in relation to their ancestral homeland and sense of ethnic identity.

Research Locations

The interview data analyzed in this book were drawn from a series of face-to-face interviews (May 2015–August 2019), along with additional online interviews conducted during the pandemic period (March–June 2021). The participants were young Canadians of ethnic Korean backgrounds. They were children of Korean immigrant families and were aged between 16 and 30. The participants were recruited through advertisements and snowballing, in which participants introduced their peer Korean Canadians to the research study. The data were collected in three Canadian locations—the Greater Toronto area, the Greater Vancouver area, and the

City of Kelowna. These locations were purposefully chosen for comparison—two Asian-populated metropolitan areas (Toronto and Vancouver) and a relatively White-dominant medium-sized city (Kelowna). Toronto and Vancouver are known as popular destinations for Asian immigrants and accordingly are known for their multiethnic populations. According to the 2016 Census (Statistics Canada 2019), the White population in Toronto and Vancouver respectively constituted 50.2% and 49.3% of the city's entire population and is anticipated to be smaller in the future. The proportions may be contrasted with that in Kelowna (86.2%), known for its White-dominant population.

Research Participants

In the 3 locations, a total of 40 young people participated in individual interviews conducted in English, which was a more comfortable language than Korean for all participants. When interview accounts are cited throughout this book, the participants' English pseudonyms are used. During the consent processes, some participants used their Korean name, but more participants used their English name. It was decided by the researcher that all participants would be named by their English pseudonyms for consistency.[3] Categorically speaking, the participants were 1.5 generation or second generation. While only 6 participants of the sample were born in Canada, more than half of the entire sample migrated to Canada in their early childhood (under the age of 8) and thus have limited affiliation with and memories of their country of birth.

---

[3] The choice between Korean and English names may be related to the ways in which the young Korean Canadians identify themselves. It is not surprising that more interview participants preferred to use their English name (regardless of their legal name) as they may prefer to be referred to that way among peers and in social settings. They might have learned to not use their Korean name to avoid potential racialization in certain circumstances because "racist incidents and microaggressions" may condition Korean Canadians to hide their Korean name (Hwang 2021). In her recent article "My Korean name is Ki Sun, and I'm choosing not to be ashamed of it anymore," the 30-year-old Korean Canadian reporter Hwang stated, "it took 30 years, but I am now ready to reclaim this part of my Korean Canadian identity." Such reclaiming of Korean names has recently been observed in media representation of diasporic Koreans. For example, in the Netflix miniseries *The Chair* (2021), the Korean American professor and chairperson title role (played by Sandra Oh) uses, and is only referred to by, her Korean name "Ji-Yoon Kim" throughout the entire series.

According to the interviewees' anecdotal accounts, young Korean Canadian experiences share certain similarities, such as racialization (which will be addressed throughout this book). However, their experiences vary depending on their context of migration and settlement (such as the age of migration and the type of family upbringing). Moreover, while diasporic Korean youth could include a wide range of young people on the move, this book only focuses on those who had (permanently) migrated to, or were otherwise born and live in, Canada. Consequently, those who are in a relatively transient or temporary state of migration have been excluded—for example international students and children of transnational Korean families, who are often referred to as goose families (in which the child, along with the mother, live in Canada for study while the father works in Korea to financially support the family in Canada).

The main aim of the recruitment process was to look for and interview young people of Korean backgrounds who regularly or frequently access transnational Korean media. The participants included a range of audience members—from highly dedicated K-pop fans to regular K-drama viewers. However, those who did not access Korean media were excluded. This excluded group includes those individuals that the interview participants referred to somewhat disapprovingly as "bananas" (i.e., people who look "yellow" but are internally "Whitewashed"), as they are relatively assimilated to the dominant White culture and thus appear to be disinterested in K-pop, K-drama, or any other made-in-Korea cultural content. The interview participants' engagement with transnational Korean media also varied depending on many factors. Some were dedicated fans while others were regular audience participants. By recruiting a range of "fan audiences," the study avoided the dichotomy between "passive audiences" and "active fans" and considered that various audience forms exist on a continuum (Jenkins et al. 2015).

In terms of their exposure to and engagement with Hallyu media, the participants show several different patterns. Overall, the interview participants were relatively familiar with Korean media and popular culture. As examined throughout the book, most of the young Korean Canadians in the study became familiar with Korean media during their upbringing in Korean immigrant families, but they did not necessarily continue their interest in Korean media. Given the interviewees' accounts, three types of young Korean Canadian audiences can be identified in terms of childhood exposure to Korean media. First, there are those who were significantly exposed to Korean media during childhood (the pre- or early Hallyu period) and later developed further their own interest in Hallyu media, such as K-pop. Second, there are those who were more or less exposed to Korean media during childhood yet lost their interest in it for a while before later developing their own interest in Hallyu as a result of motivational factors. Third, there are those who had limited exposure to pre-Hallyu Korean media and remained indifferent to Hallyu media. These different childhood experiences with Korean media (during the pre- or early Hallyu period) later evolved into different cultural tastes for more recent forms of Korean media (such as idol group-driven K-pop).

Researcher

When studying young Korean Canadians, the author's positionality as a first generation immigrant, male, middle-aged researcher may offer some limitations. There might be a clear power imbalance between the researcher who is an older Korean academic and the young people, most of whom were university students. Research into children and young people inherently involves power hierarchies between the researcher and the researched. Thus, it may be more strategic to "understand the 'between-ness' and relationality, co-dependence and constitutive force (via a nexus of power relations)" (Holland et al. 2010, p. 363). As a way of understanding the relationality between the researcher and the participants, the project involved several Korean Canadian undergraduate assistants, who supported the qualitative interviews with the young participants and provided feedback to the researcher. Despite such an effort, the researcher's positionality as a first generation immigrant may have obstructed an immersed understanding of diasporic young people's everyday lives. However, there were still common interests—Korean media and popular culture—between the researcher and the participants. The dramatic increase in Korean cultural content offered an intriguing topic to discuss together in relation to experiences of racialization in Canada. Admittedly, this book might be a set of snapshots of the interviewees' experiences and thoughts in a particular moment of their life stages while interacting with the researcher.

Contextualizing Korean Diaspora and Hallyu in Canada

Hallyu in Canada

While there have been increasing studies of various overseas reception points of Korean media, the majority address the US. It may be worth examining how Hallyu is located and localized in Canada, especially as differentiated from its southern neighbor the US, which has undeniably played a central role in leading Western media discourses about the Korean Wave (Jin et al. 2021). That is, apart from the Korean media that has been producing a large amount of (often celebratory) reports around Hallyu, the US mainstream media, as well as social media platforms, has played a significant role in gatekeeping Hallyu discourses for other overseas media and audiences. K-pop group rankings on the Billboard Hot 100 chart have often been considered as a litmus paper of their "global" recognition and success. In comparison with the US, Canada is a relatively smaller and less vibrant market for Korean media products. For example, major K-pop musicians' rankings on Canadian music charts have been typically lower than on American charts. As of September 2021, BTS's single "Butter," which was ranked #1 for 10 weeks on the American Billboard Hot 100 chart, was never ranked #1 on the Canadian Billboard Hot 100 chart (merely ranked #2 in its first week only).

Among other factors, the smaller diasporic Korean community and subsequent lack of presence of Korean culture in public discourses and media might be a factor that has restricted Hallyu's rapid flows in Canada. Indeed, the young Korean Canadians interviewed for this book commonly noted that Canada was somewhat behind the US in the introduction of Korean pop culture. While more and more K-pop concerts have been held in Toronto and Vancouver since the 2010s (except for the COVID-19 period), the young Korean Canadians in this book, especially those who were K-pop fans, lamented the limited opportunities and resources for accessing K-pop concerts and merchandise in Canada. In contrast, a significant number of major K-pop concerts, including K-CON, are held in the US, and a few interviewees made trips to the US to see their favorite idols perform. While there are limited data to estimate the impact of Hallyu in Canada, news media have reported that Korean language courses at universities are increasingly popular and often have long waitlists owing to the popular rise of K-pop among young people (Shahzad 2017).

Korean Canadians in Multiethnic Canada

To better understand young Korean Canadians and their engagement with Hallyu media in this book, it may be important to know the context of where they grew up and how their family immigrated. Canada is the most multiethnic country among the G8 (highly industrialized countries), with a foreign-born population representing 21.9% of the total Canadian population as of 2016 (Statistics Canada 2019). The foreign-born population percentage is particularly higher in Toronto and Vancouver where immigrants respectively constitute 47% and 42.5% of the total population (Statistics Canada 2019). Toronto and Vancouver have been the two most popular destinations for Korean immigrants, many of whom engage with "chain migration" (MacDonald and MacDonald 1964). Given that Korean Canadian immigrants have been involved in the ethnic economy, such as small businesses, it is not surprising that the Greater Toronto and Vancouver areas where Korean ethnic networks developed relatively early have been preferred destinations for Korean immigrants. As of 2016, more than half of ethnic Koreans in Canada live in two metropolitan areas—Vancouver (27%) and Toronto (35%) (Statistics Canada 2019). These two areas are popular destinations not only for Korean immigrants but also for other immigrants of color.

According to the 2016 Census (Statistics Canada 2019), people of Korean ethnic origin constitute 0.54% of the total Canadian population (188,710 out of 34,460,065). The Korean ethnic group is much smaller than its Chinese (1,577,060) or Filipino (780,125) counterparts, while being bigger than the Japanese population (92,920). Korean Canadians constitute a comparatively newer diasporic community, as its size has more than doubled between 1996 and 2006 (J. Park 2012). Thus, Korean communities in Canada are relatively younger especially compared to the general population. In comparison with the general Canadian population, the ethnic Korean population has been considered a "relatively young, strongly family-based, and highly educated" group (J. Park 2012, p. 34). Korean Canadians also constitute a relatively younger demographic than their counterparts in the US, where the history of Korean immigration is significantly longer. For example, Vancouver's Koreatown, located in the city's outskirts, was established in the early 2000s (Baker and DeVries 2010), which is much later than Los Angeles' Koreatown, which has substantially developed since the late 1960s and the early 1970s (Park and Kim 2008). Despite the different histories, Korean immigrants' patterns of integration into the receiving country appear to be similar in both the US and Canada. For example, studies have observed Korean immigrants' high rate of self-employment in the ethnic economy and reliance on the ethnic community in both countries (see Min and Noh 2014).

According to Kim et al. (2012), Korean immigration in Canada can be identified by several chronological waves. First, while a small number of Korean immigrants arrived in Canada after 1963 when diplomatic relations were initiated between Korea and Canada, the number remained insignificant until 1973 when the Canadian embassy was established in Korea (Kim et al. 2012). This first major wave of Korean immigration in Canada, which peaked in 1975 with 4,331 immigrants, declined due to several factors such as the Korean government's restriction of emigration of wealthy Koreans and Canada's economic recession. Another visible wave of Korean immigration was observed between the mid-1980s and the early 2000s, which was characterized by a significant inflow of business-class immigrants equipped with financial viability as entrepreneurs or in self-employment (Kim et al. 2012). According to Kim et al. (2012), the wave of Korean immigrants since 2004 is referred to as "regionalization and transnational." This new wave involves "regionalization" as province-specific immigration programs for business-class applicants have increased. Moreover, it involves "transnational" migration that includes transnational families whose members are separated for their children's overseas education in Canada and Korean international students in Canada (Jeong and Bélanger 2012).[4]

The young Korean Canadians interviewed for this book were either born in or moved to Canada between the late 1990s and the early 2010s. Thus, their migration trajectories cover the two recent waves of Korean immigration in Canada. The period since the late 1990s involves significant social transformation of Korea, beginning with the 1997 Asian financial crisis. The crisis swept away the economic fruits that Koreans had enjoyed for the previous decade and devalued the Korean currency. The crisis not only damaged Korea's national economy but also resulted in emotional shocks among Koreans, which motivated an increasing number

---

[4] The Korean transnational family usually refers to a family with a "parachute" child who studies abroad under the supervision of a legal guardian without their parents and the *kirogi gajok*, or "wild geese family," in which one parent remains in Korea while the other parent accompanies the child's study abroad (Kim et al.2012, p. 13).

of migrants, especially from the "professional class," to land in more economically stable Western countries (Kim et al. 2012, p. 11).

First generation Korean Canadians tend to be self-employed or employed in the ethnic economy, including convenience stories, ethnic restaurants, and gas stations (Chan and Fong 2012).[5] According to the 2006 Census, Korean Canadians were more self-employed compared to the general population; it is estimated that one in every four Koreans in Toronto and Vancouver are self-employed (Chan and Fong 2012). Overall, first generation Korean Canadians are more educated than the general population yet earn less than the average Canadian and experience difficulties in career mobility. Such barriers may lead first generation Korean Canadians to become entrepreneurs in the ethnic economy rather than wage earners in the general economy; in comparison, the second generations are more likely to be salary earners than to be self-employed. According to the 2006 Census, 97% of self-employed Koreans are foreign born, whereas Canadian-born Koreans are primarily wage earners (Chan and Fong 2012, p. 121).

Korean Canadian Family Experiences

The accounts of the young people interviewed for this book confirmed the first generation immigrants' under-employment and self-employment in response to difficulties with career transition in Canada. Many interviewees' families ran or worked in small businesses at the time of the interviews. Only a few interviewees' parents were professional salary earners and continued the career they had in Korea. Most of the young people recalled that their parents' migration decision had been driven by a few major reasons—most importantly, their children's education opportunities in Canada as an English-speaking, advanced country (*seonjinguk*) and better life opportunities for their families. This response resonates with H. Yoon's (2016) survey conducted in Winnipeg, Canada, in which Korean immigrants identified that children's education (44%) was the

---

[5] It is estimated that a majority of convenience stores were owned and run by Korean immigrants in Toronto and Vancouver. For example, in Vancouver, approximately 250 convenience stores were owned by Koreans in the early 2000s; however, the number is decreasing (an estimated 150 stores in 2018). Due to the expansion of large store chains, convenience stores are no longer popular small businesses for Korean immigrants in Canada, while sushi restaurants have recently become more popular (Ju 2018).

most important reason for immigration, followed by other reasons such as better quality of life (15%) and economic purposes (8%).

First generation Korean immigrants are motivated by their "Canadian dream," which could be a Canadian equivalent to the "American dream." Indeed, the US and Canada have been the two most popular destinations of Korean emigrants. For example, in 2018, when 6,330 Koreans migrated to another country, the US was the top destination (3,223 emigrants), followed by Canada (1,092 emigrants); the two countries were followed by Australia (547) and New Zealand (255) (e-narajipyo 2021). Koreans' pursuit of the Canadian dream has been examined in a few studies, such as K. Yoon's (2014) study, in which young Koreans considered Canada an ideal "global" location to live. Canada has been a globally popular destination and has received a substantial number of immigrants each year. In 2016, Canada had 296,379 new permanent residents and was ranked fourth in terms of annual intake, behind the US (1,183,505), Germany (1,051,014), and the United Kingdom (350,085) (Organisation for Economic Co-operation and Development 2020).

Recent migration from Korea to Canada especially after the 1990s has been triggered by motivations for education and lifestyle (H. Yoon 2016). H. Yoon (2016) has claimed that neoliberal global economy concerns are both pull and push factors for Koreans' immigration in Canada. In particular, Korean immigrants seek to avoid the highly neoliberalized, competitive Korean society by moving to an advanced Western country, such as Canada, which represents seemingly better lifestyles and educational infrastructure. As many Korean immigrants in Canada are involved in the ethnic economy, comprised of Korean restaurants, grocery and convenience stores, and other small businesses, ethnic enclaves have developed in the downtown or outskirts of large Canadian cities (such as Toronto and Vancouver), which are often referred to as Koreatown. These areas have contributed to the dissemination of Korean popular culture and media to some extent. In particular, Korean restaurants often play K-pop as background music or have K-pop music videos on TV, and thus immerse Canadian customers in Hallyu. Moreover, Korean entrepreneurs contribute to, or organize, Hallyu-related events (J. Kim 2018).

The histories and geographies of Koreans' immigration in Canada may influence the upbringing of the children of Korean immigrants. The young people grow up in families primarily involved in small businesses and the ethnic economy rather than those integrated into the general economy. The relatively short history and small size of the

Korean community in Canada, as well as its detachment from the general economy, affect the ways in which younger generations think about their ethnic identity as they engage with K-pop, Korean TV and films, and other Hallyu media while growing up in Canada.

SIGNIFICANCE AND ORGANIZATION OF THE BOOK

Why Diasporic Hallyu?

Diasporic flows of media from the homeland may not be a new phenomenon. Many diasporic communities and individuals seek to access media and cultural forms from their left-behind (ancestral) homeland (Georgiou 2006). However, while diasporic media consumption has typically been led by first generation immigrants, who prefer media forms from their homeland or ethnic language media (Georgiou 2006), the recent social media-driven flows of the Korean Wave have reached out beyond national or ethnic boundaries.

Despite increasing audience studies on the reception of Korean pop culture in Asia and elsewhere, the diasporic populations involved in the production, circulation, and consumption of this new cultural flow have remained a grey area. As has been observed in recent books on the Korean Wave (Y. Kim 2013; Lee and Nornes 2015; Yoon and Jin 2017), researchers of audience studies may have been intrigued primarily by "pop cosmopolitans" (Jenkins 2004; Jenkins et al. 2013), rather than diasporic audiences. While Hallyu extends beyond the ethnic audiences' consumption of their homeland media, its increasing penetration into non-Korean populations may not be fully examined without exploring the role of Korean diasporic communities in facilitating the Korean Wave. Given the importance of diasporic Korean audiences of the Korean Wave—those who have not been sufficiently examined in the existing studies—this book analyzes how they engage with the transnational flows of the Korean Wave. This book's unique focus on and in-depth study of diasporic Korean audiences addresses a lacuna in the existing studies of the Korean Wave—that is, the role of the Korean diaspora in the transnational flows of Korean media and popular culture. Drawing on extensive audience studies and empirical analyses, the book proposes a critical understanding of diasporic audiences who reorient the dominant mediascape by consuming transnational media forms of non-Western origin in between "here" (location of residence) and "there" (ethnic homeland). This evidence-based, in-depth analysis of diasporic audiences' media practices expands the scope of existing studies of the Korean Wave and furthermore suggests a new perspective on audience research.

Since diaspora is a way of imagining borders, groups, and individuals dealing with cultural difference, the analytical framework of diaspora can contribute to advancing Hallyu audience studies. Moreover, the diasporic lens utilized in this book can be further applied to analyze a wide range of contemporary young people and their engagement with transnational media. The diasporic framework helps to explore how young people engage with the multiple cultural identifications that are available for them in the midst of transnational cultural flows. This book expands the scope of transnational audience studies, which has insufficiently examined diasporic media practices among people in between two or more cultural contexts. The book also advances Korean Wave studies, which still primarily address transactions between culture, technology, and people from a nation-statistic perspective.

Organization of the Book

This book consists of theoretical and empirical chapters. This chapter and Chapter 5 offer the theoretical frameworks and contexts for the research, and Chapters 2–4 engage with the findings of qualitative interviews with young Korean Canadians.

This chapter provides the context and framework for the book. By acknowledging that the diasporic population has remained an under-researched area in Korean Wave studies, the chapter addresses why diasporic youth are important for understanding the Korean Wave beyond a nation-statist perspective. The chapter offers an overview of the recent circulation of transnational Korean media and delineates the book's research contexts by describing the research participants and a brief history of Korean Canadian communities.

Chapter 2 addresses how diasporic Korean youth in Canada grow up with an understanding of their cultural differences. In particular, young Korean Canadians often feel that they are subject to (and have to be validated by) the dominant cultural norms of White Anglo groups at least for a period in their childhood, while later developing more positive ethnic identification. In their transition to adulthood, during which they try to negotiate their available ethnic options and explore what it means to be

Korean *and* Canadian, Hallyu media seems to offer cultural resources for exploring who they are.

Chapter 3 focuses on young Korean Canadians' viewing of and engagement with narrative Korean media genres (Korean TV dramas, entertainment shows, and vlogs). Their diasporic viewing of Korean TV reveals how the Korean Wave is integrated into viewers' everyday contexts. In the midst of White-dominant media representation, the increasing global popularity of Korean TV may provide the diasporic youth with meaningful momentum for exploring how they can critically navigate between different cultural texts and contexts.

Drawing on the diasporic young people's consumption and understanding of K-pop, Chapter 4 examines the particular meanings that are generated as these youth engage with K-pop in the process of growing up. In particular, the chapter examines how K-pop is interpreted not only as an ethnic cultural text but also as a global cultural text. Moreover, it addresses how K-pop is appropriated by diasporic youth as a cultural resource for challenging the White-dominant cultural frame.

In wrapping up the themes of the book, Chapter 5 suggests that Hallyu media itself may not be inherently counter-hegemonic, but diasporic audiences' critical engagement with the cultural wave may enhance its potential to challenge the dominant Western-centric mediascape. The chapter also claims that diasporic youth learn and negotiate different identity positions, associated with here *and* there, through Hallyu media.

References

Ahn, Ji-Hyun, and E. Kyung Yoon. 2020. Between love and hate: The New Korean Wave, Japanese female fans, and anti-Korean sentiment in Japan. *Journal of Contemporary Eastern Asia* 19 (2): 179–196.

Anderson, Benedict. 1998. *The spectre of comparisons: Nationalism, Southeast Asia, and the world*. London: Verso.

Baker, Don, and Larry DeVries. 2010. Introduction. In *Asian religions in British Columbia*, ed. Larry DeVries, Don Baker, and Dan Overmyer, 1–14. Vancouver: University of British Columbia Press.

Bhabha, Homi K. 1994. *The location of culture*. London: Routledge.

Brah, Avtar. 1996. *Cartographies of diaspora: Contesting identities*. London: Routledge.

Brubaker, Rogers. 2005. The "diaspora" diaspora. *Ethnic and Racial Studies* 28 (1): 1–19.

Chan, Elic, and Eric Fong. 2012. Social, economic, and demographic characteristics of Korean self-employment in Canada. In *Korean immigrants in Canada: Perspectives on migration, integration, and the family*, ed. Samuel Noh, Ann H. Kim, and Marianne S. Noh, 115–132. Toronto: University of Toronto Press.

Chin, Bertha, and Lori Hitchcock Morimoto. 2013. Towards a theory of transcultural fandom. *Participations* 10 (1): 92–108.

Colombo, Enzo. 2014. Living on the move: Belonging and identification among adolescent children of immigrants in Italy. In *Migration, diaspora and identity: Cross-national experiences*, ed. Georgina Tsolidis, 19–35. New York: Springer.

Colombo, Enzo, and Paola Rebughini. 2012. *Children of immigrants in a globalized world: A generational experience*. New York: Palgrave.

Choi, Jungbong, and Roald Maliangkay. 2015. Introduction: Why fandom matters to the international rise of K-pop. In *K-pop: The international rise of the Korean music industry*, ed. Jungbong Choi and Roald Maliangkay, 1–18. London: Routledge.

Chua, Beng Huat, and Koichi Iwabuchi, eds. 2008. *East Asian pop culture: Analysing the Korean Wave*. Hong Kong: Hong Kong University Press.

Danico, Mary Yu. 2004. *The 1.5 Generation: Becoming Korean American in Hawaii*. Honolulu: University of Hawaii Press.

E-narajipyo. 2021. Statistics on overseas emigration. https://www.index.go.kr/potal/main/EachDtlPageDetail.do?idx_cd=1684 [in Korean].

Feldman, Gregory. 2015. *We are all migrants*. Stanford: Stanford University Press.

García Canclini, Néstor. 2000. State of hybridization. In *Without guarantees: In honour of Stuart Hall*, ed. Paul Giloy, Lawrence Grossberg, and Angela McRobbie, 38–52. New York: Verso.

Georgiou, Myria. 2006. *Diaspora, identity and the media: Diasporic transnationalism and mediated spatialities*. New York: Hampton Press.

Gigi Durham, Meenakshi. 2004. Constructing the "new ethnicities": Media, sexuality, and diaspora identity in the lives of South Asian immigrant girls. *Critical Studies in Media Communication* 21 (2): 140–161.

Han, Benjamin. 2017. K-pop in Latin America: Transcultural fandom and digital mediation. *International Journal of Communication* 11: 2250–2269.

Holland, Sally, Emma Renold, Nicola J. Ross, and Alexandra Hillman. 2010. Power, agency and participatory agendas: A critical exploration of young people's engagement in participative qualitative research. *Childhood* 17 (3): 360–375.

Hu, Brian. 2010. Korean TV serials in the English-language diaspora: Translating difference online and making it racial. *The Velvet Light Trap* 66: 36–49.

Hwang, Priscilla Ki Sun. 2021. My Korean name is Ki Sun, and I'm choosing not to be ashamed of it anymore. *CBC News*, May 25. https://www.cbc.ca/news/canada/ottawa/reclaiming-my-korean-name-first-person-1.6027338.

Jeong, Jumin, and Daniele Bélanger. 2012. *Kirogi* families as virtual "families": Perspectives and experiences of *kirogi* mothers. In *Korean immigrants in Canada: Perspectives on migration, integration, and the family*, ed. Samuel Noh, Ann H. Kim, and Marianne S. Noh, 259–284. Toronto: University of Toronto Press.

Jenkins, Henry. 2004. Pop cosmopolitanism: Mapping cultural flows in an age of media convergence. In *Globalization: Culture and education in the new millennium*, ed. Marcelo Suárez-Orozco and Desirée B. Qin-Hilliard, 114–140. Berkeley: University of California Press.

Jenkins, Henry, Sam Ford, and Joshua Green. 2013. *Spreadable media: Creating value and meaning in a networked culture*. New York: New York University Press.

Jenkins, Henry, Mizuko Ito, and danah boyd. 2015. *Participatory culture in a networked era: A Conversation on youth, learning, commerce, and politics*. Cambridge: Polity.

Jin, Dal Yong. 2016. *New Korean Wave: Transnational cultural power in the age of social media*. Champaign: University of Illinois Press.

Jin, Dal Yong. 2018. The Korean government's new cultural policy in the age of social media. In *Asian cultural flows: Cultural policies, creative industries, and media consumers*, ed. Nobuko Kawashima and Hye-Kyung Lee, 3–17. New York: Palgrave.

Jin, Dal Yong, Kyong Yoon, and Wonjung Min. 2021. *Transnational Hallyu: The Globalization of Korean digital and popular culture*. Lanham: Rowman & Littlefield.

Ju, Hoseok. 2018. Sushi restaurants and motels are emerging as popular businesses instead of convenience stores among Korean immigrants in Canada. *JoongAng Ilbo*, May 8. https://www.joongang.co.kr/article/22601942#home [in Korean].

Kalra, Virinder, Raminder Kaur, and John Hutnyk. 2005. *Diaspora and hybridity*. London: Sage.

Kim, Gooyong. 2018. *From factory girls to K-pop idol girls: Cultural politics of developmentalism, patriarchy, and neoliberalism in South Korea's popular music industry*. Lanham: Lexington.

Kim, Jinwon. 2018. Manhattan's Koreatown as a transclave: The emergence of a new ethnic enclave in a global city. *City & Community* 17 (1): 276–295.

Kim, Suk-Young. 2018. *K-pop live: Fans, idols, and multimedia performance*. Stanford: Stanford University Press.

Kim, Youna, ed. 2013. *The Korean Wave: Korean media go global*. London: Routledge.

Kim, Ann H., Samuel Noh, and Marianne S. Noh. 2012. Introduction: Historical context and contemporary research. In *Korean immigrants in Canada: Perspectives on migration, integration, and the family*, ed. Samuel Noh, Ann H. Kim, and Marianne S. Noh, 1–18. Toronto: University of Toronto Press.

Koh, Ho Youn, and Kyungmin Baek. 2020. The Korean diasporic identity in the context of K-pop consumption. *Journal of Asian Sociology* 49 (1): 1–28.

Korea Foundation for International Cultural Exchange. 2012. *The annual survey of overseas Hallyu*. Seoul: Korea Foundation for International Cultural Exchange (KOFICE) [in Korean].

Kuwahara, Yasue, ed. 2014. *The Korean Wave: Korean popular culture in global context*. New York: Palgrave.

Lee, Hyangjin. 2017. The Korean Wave and anti-Korean Wave sentiment in Japan. In *The Korean Wave: Evolution, fandom, and transnationality*, ed. Tae-Jin Yoon and Dal Yong Jin, 185–208. Lanham: Lexington Books.

Lee, Sangjoon, and Abé Markus Nornes, ed. 2015. *Hallyu 2.0: The Korean Wave in the age of social media*. Ann Arbor: University of Michigan Press.

Liew, Kendrea 2021. Future of entertainment? Avatars could be K-pop's next superstars. https://www.cnbc.com/2021/01/11/future-of-entertainment-avatars-could-be-k-pops-next-superstars.html.

Nye, Joseph, and Youna Kim. 2013. Soft power and the Korean Wave. In *The Korean Wave: Korean media go global*, ed. Youna Kim, 31–42. London: Routledge.

MacDonald, John S., and Leatrice D. MacDonald. 1964. Chain migration ethnic neighborhood formation and social networks. *The Milbank Memorial Fund Quarterly* 42 (1): 82–97.

Min, Pyong Gap, and Samuel Noh, eds. 2014. *Second-generation Korean experiences in the United States and Canada*. Lanham: Lexington Books.

Organisation for Economic Co-operation and Development (OECD). 2020. International migration database. https://stats.oecd.org/Index.aspx?DataSetCode=MIG.

Oh, David C. 2015. *Second-generation Korean Americans and transnational media: Diasporic identifications*. Lanham: Lexington Books.

Oh, Youjeong. 2018. *Pop city: Korean popular culture and the selling of place*. Ithaca: Cornell University Press.

Park, Jungwee. 2012. A demographic profile of Koreans in Canada. In *Korean immigrants in Canada: Perspectives on migration, integration, and the family*, ed. Samuel Noh, Ann H. Kim, and Marianne S. Noh, 19–34. Toronto: University of Toronto Press.

Park, Jung-Sun. 2013. Negotiating identity and power in transnational cultural consumption: Korean American youths and the Korean Wave. In *The Korean Wave: Korean media go global*, ed. Youna Kim, 136–150. London: Routledge.

Park, Kyeyoung, and Jessica Kim. 2008. The contested nexus of Los Angeles Koreatown: Capital restructuring, gentrification, and displacement. *Amerasia Journal* 34 (3): 127–150.

Robinson, Douglas. 1997. *Translation and empire*. London: Routledge.

Rumbaut, Rubén G. 2012. Generation 1.5, educational experiences of. In *Encyclopedia of diversity in education*, ed. James A. Banks, 983, London: Sage.

Ryoo, Woongjae. 2009. Globalization, or the logic of cultural hybridization: The case of the Korean Wave. *Asian Journal of Communication* 19 (2): 137–151.

Sakamoto, Rumi, and Matthew Allen. 2007. "Hating 'The Korean Wave'" comic books: A sign of new nationalism in Japan? *The Asia-Pacific Journal: Japan Focus* 5 (1): 1–16. https://apjjf.org/-Rumi-SAKAMOTO/2535/art icle.html.

Shahzad, Ramna. 2017. Here's the unexpected reason why Korean language courses are so popular at U of T. *CBC News*, 13 March. https://www.cbc.ca/news/canada/toronto/programs/metromorning/korean-interst-1.4022395.

Statistics Canada. 2019. Census profile, 2016 Census. https://www12.statcan.gc.ca/census-recensement/2016/dp-pd/prof/index.cfm?Lang=E.

Walsh, John. 2014. Hallyu as a government construct: The Korean Wave in the context of economic and social development. In *The Korean Wave: Korean popular culture in global context*, ed. Yasue Kuwahara, 13–31. New York: Palgrave.

Yoon, Hyejin. 2016. Family strategies in a neoliberal world: Korean immigrants in Winnipeg. *GeoJournal* 81 (2): 243–256.

Yoon, Kyong. 2014. Transnational youth mobility in the neoliberal economy of experience. *Journal of Youth Studies* 17 (8): 1014–1028.

Yoon, Kyong. 2020. Diasporic Korean audiences of Hallyu in Vancouver Canada. *Korea Journal* 60 (1): 152–178.

Yoon, Tae-Jin, and Dal Yong Jin, ed. 2017. *The Korean Wave: Evolution, fandom, and transnationality*. Lanham: Lexington Books.

Yoon, Tae-Jin, and Bora Kang. 2017. Emergence, evolution and extension of "Hallyu Studies": What have scholars found from Korean pop culture in the last twenty years? In *The Korean Wave: Evolution, fandom, and transnationality*, ed. Tae-Jin Yoon and Dal Yong Jin, 3–21. Lanham: Lexington Books.

CHAPTER 2

Growing Up Korean Canadian in the Time of the Korean Wave

Abstract Diasporic Korean youth in Canada grow up while realizing their cultural differences. Their awareness of difference often limits the scope of their possible lives. They internalize the White-dominant cultural frame that presents a view of themselves as the other. Young Korean Canadians feel that they are subject to (and have to be validated by) the dominant cultural norms of White Anglo groups at least for a period in their childhood, and later in life they develop more positive ethnic identification. As these young people grow up, they try to explore and negotiate their ethnic options and what it means to be Korean *and* Canadian. In this process of growing up, transnational Korean media offers the diasporic Korean youth cultural resources for exploring who they are in between different identity positions.

Keywords The Korean Wave (Hallyu) · Diasporic youth · Ethnic identification · Racialization · Stereotyping · White-dominant cultural frame

In a recent interview, Hanmin Yang, a young Korean Canadian IT startup entrepreneur (and the founder of the Asian-specific dating app Alike), shared his experiences of growing up in Toronto as a child of a Korean immigrant family. He spoke about the identity crisis that he faced as a child of a minority background since his landing in Canada at the age of 8.

© The Author(s) 2022
K. Yoon, *Diasporic Hallyu*, East Asian Popular Culture,
https://doi.org/10.1007/978-3-030-94964-8_2

> I failed to identify what I was and how I fit in. I didn't know how I perceived myself because I was thrown into this thing. From the moment that I arrived, I wanted to find how I fit in this picture. Where's my place? What am I? How do others see me? It was difficult because I didn't have a sense of self-identity of my own. So, I think I relied heavily on how others saw me. And because of that, I put on airs and I acted bigger than I was. That was always in my mind. What am I? How do other people see me? What is the right way to behave? And I think others saw me as some sort of small geeky Korean kid who's good at school. (BeyondAsian 2020)

Yang's struggle growing up as a Korean Canadian reveals how minority youth have been treated in Canada, where multiculturalism was adopted as an official policy as early as the 1970s. In the interview, he speaks about a coming-of-age journey to explore Korean Canadian identity and the struggle to move beyond the pervasive stereotypes of Asian people in Canada. This retrospective account seems to still be relevant for understanding today's Korean Canadian youth.

Yang's story is echoed in the accounts of many young Korean Canadians interviewed for this book. The interview participants shared their experiences of growing up, especially in association with the pervasive racialization of Asians in their schools and neighborhoods. Some admitted that they had not felt "fully Canadian" at some moments in their childhood. Despite their Canadian citizenship and education in Canada, several interviewees separated themselves from the category of Canadian. For example, speaking about his school days, Lucas, a 24-year-old recent university graduate, described his White classmates as "Canadians" in comparison with non-Whites who were often addressed with ethnic identifiers such as "Korean" and "Chinese." Like Lucas, some interviewees were not free of the White-dominant culture in which White people represent "Canadians" without a particular identifier while non-Whites are positioned as the racialized other of society (Henry and Tator 2010).

This chapter addresses how the recent rise of the Korean Wave (or Hallyu) may be integrated into Korean Canadians' identity work in their transition to adulthood, especially in relation to their responses to the White-dominant cultural frame that has taken the White Anglo culture for granted as the default cultural mode constituting Canadian culture. Recent Hallyu media may be different from other examples of diasporic cultural flows, such as the Bollywood cinema popular in Indian diasporas, because Hallyu is far more extensively circulated beyond diasporic audiences who are culturally and linguistically proximal to the cultural texts. In the latest phase of Hallyu, known as the "New Korean Wave" (since the 2010s), which does not necessarily target culturally proximal audiences, diasporic youth's engagement with Hallyu does not simply mean the nostalgic consumption of ethnic language media but involves complicated audience experiences. In particular, young Korean Canadians receive transnational Korean media not only as inherited cultural texts rooted in their ancestral homeland but also as highly hybrid cultural texts.

This chapter begins by discussing how young Korean Canadians feel or do not feel fully Canadian and what it means to be fully Canadian. By reflecting on their experiences of racialization in childhood and adolescence, the young people interviewed for this book reveal how seemingly multicultural Canada shapes the identity positions of young people of color and immigrant backgrounds. The chapter situates the rise of Hallyu in diasporic young people's everyday contexts and negotiation of diasporic identities. Drawing on in-depth interviews with young people of Korean heritage in Canada, the chapter explores how young Korean Canadians engage with Hallyu in their transition to adulthood in response to the White-dominant cultural frame that is still experienced by many youth of color in the seemingly multicultural society of Canada (Henry and Tator 2010).

RACIALIZED YOUTH

What is it like growing up as a Korean Canadian? Empirical studies of young Koreans of immigrant backgrounds have revealed that they grow up as racialized subjects and are under the pressure of assimilation. As existing studies in North America have shown, in comparison with their White peers, the diasporic Korean youth are often racialized, marginalized, and "tolerated" as the other in (and of) the "host" population—White settlers (Danico 2004; Kibria 2002; D. Y. Kim 2013; Oh 2015). As Yang's anecdote above implies, young people of color appear to experience unstable, ambivalent feelings of belonging. Experiences of racialization were observed among the accounts of the young people interviewed for this book. Growing up, they became aware that their family was "different" and that they were different according to the White-dominant cultural frame. They learned to see themselves as racialized others according to the lens of the White Canadians.

Growing Up "Different"

In schools and public spaces, the Korean Canadian youth were constantly reminded that their immigrant families were different from those of their White peers, and thus often felt tensions between the cultural atmospheres of their home and the outside. Many interviewees admitted they felt confusion about their cultural identities between their Korean immigrant families and the White-dominant cultural norms that they encountered outside the home. Ben, a 21-year-old student who immigrated at the age of 5, recalled:

> At school, I was being shaped to be the ideal Western individual but at home I was raised to be the ideal Korean individual. Because of that mix, in my mind, it's just impossible to be fully integrated or fully successful in the Canadian society.

The young Korean Canadians grew up thinking that their family was foreign and might not fully belong to Canada. They learned to think about themselves as marginal subjects rather than an insider of Canadian society. Regardless of their age of immigration (or even whether they were born in Canada or not), most of the young Korean Canadians in this book had experiences of realizing their home culture as foreign or the other of mainstream Canadian culture. For example, Blake, a 26-year-old schoolteacher in Toronto, who immigrated at the age of 4, recalled an occasion in Grade 2 when he was invited to his White friend's residence and felt embarrassed about his lack of particular cultural knowledge.

> I was eating spaghetti with him. His dad was a cop, and they were a White family. I didn't know how to eat spaghetti. It was my first time even eating spaghetti. I remember his mom was like (making a gesture) "This is how you eat it." It was almost embarrassing that I didn't know how to eat it. After that point, I was thinking, "Well, this is how you eat if you are Canadian."

This way, the young Korean Canadians were reminded that they might not be fully Canadian and thus they built anxiety about their otherness or marginality as a person of color in White Canada.

Although all the young people interviewed were permanent residents or citizens in Canada, they tended to show ambivalent feelings about their sense of belonging to Canada. "I do still think I'm sort of a minority.

It's something that you can't just get rid of no matter how long you stay here," stated Nicole, a 26-year-old professional born in Seoul yet raised primarily in Vancouver. After immigrating to Vancouver during her elementary school period, she studied and worked hard to integrate into Canadian society. Different from her parents' generation (first generation immigrants), who had limited access to the general economy such as the public sectors and mainstream industry sectors, Nicole successfully landed in a public sector job soon after graduation. However, she saw herself as only partially Canadian. Many young people interviewed for this book spoke about their restricted sense of belonging to Canadian society. Such feelings were more evident among those who were born in Korea and moved to Canada during their childhood rather than those who were born in Canada; however, the latter (second generation) also expressed their ambivalent sense of belonging to Canada. Regardless of their age of migration or birthplace, most of the interviewees, explicitly or implicitly, felt like "forever foreigners" who remain on the margins of the White-dominant society, to some extent (Tuan 1998; Zhou 2004).

Most of the interviewees' shared experiences of racialization resonate with Kim et al.'s (2014) survey of adolescents in Toronto, conducted in 1997 and 1998, in which 92% of Korean Canadian respondents reported encountering at least one experience of discrimination related to their ethnicity such as being insulted or called names (83.7%), experiencing rude behaviors (79.3%), having family members discriminated against (68.2%), and being treated unfairly (52.6%). In the same survey, 75.3% of other ethnic minorities and 50% of White adolescents reported such an experience. These forms of discriminatory experiences, which were also echoed in the accounts of the young people interviewed for this book, reportedly could result in mental health problems.[1] Experiences of racial discrimination sometimes begin at a very early age (even before they were aware of the concept of racism). Especially those who immigrated at the beginning of school age encountered the gaze and prejudice of others on their difference, which later they were able to interpret and

---

[1] Experiences of racialization adversely affect the mental health and self-esteem of Korean Canadian youth as shown by Kim et al.'s (2014) study. They found that Korean Canadian youth, compared to White and even other minority youth, show a much higher rate of depressive symptoms; this result also resonates with findings in previous studies of Korean American adolescents (Hovey et al. 2006; Seol et al. 2016).

articulate as racism. In several interviewees' recollections, their experiences of discrimination and stigmatization occurred as early as in their daycare. For example, 16-year-old Sherry, who immigrated to Kelowna, a predominately White-populated city, at the age of 3, recalled her feelings and interactions with others in early childhood: "There was this one place I would go to for day care and there was a lot of discrimination that happened just purely because I was Asian. They just always isolated me. All the time!" In comparison, several other interviewees realized racial discrimination relatively later in their childhood and adolescence—especially after the elementary school period. For example, 21-year-old university student Paige, who was born in Canada, recalled, "In Elementary, I don't think I ever felt different. I was like 'you're my friend and you're also my friend.' But as I got older, I feel like I can get discriminated because of my race."

Through the White Lens

According to the interviewees, growing up was a process of racialization and a struggle to "fit in." During this time, they seemed to learn how to see themselves through a White-dominant frame of reference. The young Korean Canadians' experiences of racialization often occurred in their interaction with White peers, some of whom made negative comments on their skin color, appearance, and/or food. Common examples included insulting comments such as "why are your eyes so small?" and "why does your lunch smell so stinky?" For example, Mia, an 18-year-old high school student who immigrated to Canada at the age of 3, recalled, "[while growing up] I felt really disconnected with kids in Canada because I was different from them. Usually they would point out like, 'Oh, why is your food weird?'" Similarly, 28-year-old second generation Ethan, who grew up in Toronto, described (like many other interviewees) how he had to be cautious about and ashamed of his lunch: "we [i.e., Korean Canadian kids] were almost hiding our Korean identity. In elementary school, if I brought *kimchi*, it was kind of like, eat it, cover it up, eat it, and cover it up. It's because we got made fun of." Reportedly, children of color in Canada are bullied in the lunchroom because of their lunchboxes packed with "ethnic" foods. This phenomenon has been called "lunchroom racism" (White 2011). Whether or not they immediately articulated the experiences as racism, most of the interviewees learned that they were treated differently and as the other of their White peers. Thus, they felt "insecure," "shameful," or "uncomfortable" because of their ethnic background. Several interviewees recalled that they wished they were White for a period of time when they were younger.

Being Asian in Canada brought feelings of being on the margin for most of the young people interviewed for this book. Interviewees recalled that they had perceived themselves as different from their White Anglo peers. 19-year-old university student Grace, who used to be a writer-wannabe, had considered White Anglo characters as the default of character creation: "I wanted to become a writer when I was younger. And I felt that if I had to write stories or a novel I had to write only White people with White names like Sarah Finnegan or something like that. I felt that because there just weren't any Asian names in books." Even those who grew up in Asian-populated large cities, such as Toronto and Vancouver, and thus did not feel exposed to harsh racism in their school days, were subject to pervasive stereotypes of Asians in school. 19-year-old Beth in Toronto stated, "I definitely think that as an Asian there's less racism than there are toward other races here. Maybe one problem is people expect you [as an Asian] to be better at school." That is, even those who recollected few racial discriminatory experiences were still exposed to stereotypes of and expectations about Asian people as a "model minority" in Canadian society. As addressed in Hanmin Yang's anecdote above, young Korean Canadians' constant awareness of stereotypes against them influenced how they behaved and thought about themselves. Indeed, Rosie, a 21-year-old second generation student, recalled, "I used to have this weird feeling that if I was in a room with many White people and I felt kind of uncomfortable... I look so different from them and I felt like they were judging me for it."

Overall, experiences of racialization, such as those experienced by the young Korean Canadians, are incorporated into the process of socialization through which children learn the cultural values of their society and position themselves in society as they are growing up and transitioning to adulthood. While Canadian public schooling embraces (liberal) multiculturalism, the students of color were not free of the discourse of Whiteness-as-norm, which may be reproduced through the hidden curriculum of schools—a curriculum that is taught without being formally ascribed (Ghosh 2008; Henry and Tator 2010; Moodley 1998). As a result, both White and non-White youth (and the mainstream society) accept Whiteness as the "norm" (i.e., the standard by which others should be validated), for instance when Nicole thought she had to create White characters as the default in writing fiction rather than characters of her own ethnicity. Indeed, many interviewees recalled that they tried to "fit in" and conform to the White-dominantpeer culture during their childhood, whereas they later realized that they did not have to rely on the discourse of Whiteness-as-norm (Bonilla-Silva 2017). The dominant discourse and institutions of socialization appear to not treat Whites as an ethno-racial category because they are constructed as "normal"; in contrast, non-Whites are constantly essentialized as racialized groups (Bonilla-Silva 2017; Lewis 2004). This process of socialization and schooling may serve to reproduce subtle racism through which children learned to accept and internalize the dominant understanding of races (Henry and Tator 2010). As illustrated by the interviewees' experiences, diasporic young people's identity work was subject to pervasive racialization through which they learned to see themselves as the other of the White-centric society. Indeed, many interviewees explicitly or implicitly spoke about their limited sense of belonging to Canada as *Korean* Canadians, along with a troubling sense of built-in shame and marginality as people on the margin.

Negotiating Identity, Living in Canada

Strategies of Negotiating Racialization

The racialized youth in this book struggled to "fit in" and to negotiate their situations and ethno-racial identity. In their recollections of growing up in Canada, some young people desired to be *fully Canadian*, which in fact meant to be White, at least for a certain period of their childhood and adolescence. To "fit in" and to be "fully Canadian," the young people hid their Korean ethnic identity especially during their childhood and adolescence. Some asked their parents to pack a type of lunch that the majority of their White peers would have, whereas some young women would dye their hair blonde to look like White kids. Even after having grown up, some young Korean Canadians still tried to hide their ethnic identity sometimes. For example, Olivia, a 19-year-old university student in Toronto, who immigrated at the age of 9, was worried about the disadvantages related to using her legal, Korean name.

When I put my name on my resumes it's always Olivia. I never put my legal (Korean) name because, well, I don't know. I want to believe that there is no ethnic discrimination, but I think there is more or less. (…) Like there's always that chance of getting an interview after knowing that you're Canadian. Um, instead of just you know, having your resume thrown out at first glance after seeing your name.

Olivia admitted that the use of her English name can contribute to defining her as fully Canadian without signaling her ethnic attributes. She was aware that non-English-sounding names might not be welcomed in the labor market.[2] Rosie, who grew up in Vancouver, also admitted how she had had low expectations in her job hunting, due to her ethnic background and others' stereotypes against it, until she finally got a job in a White-dominant workplace.

When I applied to work at a large popular coffee shop, I have this mindset, like, "Oh, they're probably not going to hire me" because I hadn't seen that many Asian people working there while I was there. (…) But, I applied and made it. I did turn out to be the only Asian kid [working] in the whole store.

The young Korean Canadians in this book gradually learned how to negotiate and position their ethnic identity on a personal or interpersonal level when growing up. In response to childhood (and indeed lifelong) racialization, the young people negotiated their ethnic attributes. Their common responses included distancing themselves from their ethnic culture—"ethnic disidentification" (Kibria 2002)—and/or developing further ties with their ethnic culture—"ethnic identification (Oh 2015). That is, under the pressure of assimilation, diasporic youth may initially desire to be like the dominant White group and thus seek ethnic disidentification.[3] More specifically, young Korean Canadians may oscillate between different "individualized ethnic options," such as (a)

[2] Such discrimination exists in Canada as proven by Oreopoulos's (2011) experiment in 2009 of sending 12,910 mock resumes in response to 3,255 job postings in Toronto, Canada. The experiment revealed that the percentage for receiving a callback from employers was 4.4% higher for resumes with English-sounding names than those with non-English sounding names.

[3] Furthermore, Oh (2015, pp. 24–25) identified five different positions observed among young Korean Americans—hostility to one's diasporic identity, lack of interest in one's diasporic identity, curiosity about one's diasporic identity, explicit bicultural identifications,

adherence to dominant norms of behavior, (b) opting out of an ethnic group, and (c) partial identification (Song 2003). D. Y. Kim's (2013) study of Korean American youth found that the young people, albeit rather unintentionally and ambiguously, navigate between four identity choices as immigrant (Korean), ethnic American (Korean American), pan-Asian (Asian American), and American. Overall, the previous studies confirmed that diasporic young people's ethnic identification is influenced by social contexts and interactions with others and increase/decrease throughout their transition to adulthood.

Many young people interviewed for this book tried to deny or hide their ethnic identity, at least for a short period, yet later (in high school and university) as they were transitioning to adulthood, they engaged more with their ethnic identity. George, a 20-year-old university student who left Korea at the age of 8 and was raised in a White-populated neighborhood in Kingston, a medium-sized city, described how his ways of self-identification changed at a university located in Toronto and known for its multiethnic student body.

> I'm more Korean than Canadian. But, I was kind of confused because…
> I was more like "um is this right?" Because when I was in high school,
> I mostly hung out with non-Asian, non-Korean people. I lived in a city
> called Kingston where a lot of people are Caucasian. So, I would place
> myself not super Korean but not super White, I guess (laughs). But like,
> the University of Toronto changed me a lot, because there are so many
> Koreans, so it's only natural for me to hang out with Korean people. So,
> it is only natural for me to learn about K-pop, talk in Korean, my Korean
> actually improved when I came here [Toronto], surprisingly.

For George, and many other interviewees, transition to university was a significant moment to socialize with many other Korean and Asian peers, and in so doing, to learn to overcome the internalized desire to "fit in." As Maira (2002) noted, ethnic or diasporic young people tend to "come out" as ethnic subjects during the college period (Maira 2002, p. 189), so that they learned to see themselves not necessarily through their White peers' gazes.

---

and heavy involvement in one's diasporic identity. That is, diasporic youth may oscillate between ethnic identification and disidentification, while sometimes having multiple senses of belonging.

Ethnic identification is a way of taking refuge in one's ethnic identity (D. Y. Kim 2014) or creating a symbolic home (N. Y. Kim 2018). Especially for those who were born and raised in Canada and thus do not have any embodied memories of an ancestral homeland, ethnic identification requires time, media, and effort. In this regard, as discussed in the next two chapters, the recent rise of Hallyu seems to play an increasingly important role in the second generation's development of ethnic identification. Diasporic youth's ethnic identification is also influenced by those with whom they hang out in school and in their neighborhoods—potentially Korean, Asian, non-Asian, and/or White peers. The aforementioned George described how he had difficulty managing White *and* Korean friendships simultaneously.

> In grade 12, I started to hang out with a lot of Korean people, because first time in grade 12 I found that there are some high school students who are Korean, so I started hanging out with them. And then, my other friends got really angry at me because, I would never, like, hanging out with them, and, I think there was a frustration for myself that like, I can't keep up with - I can't do both. So, I think it was either choose between these two groups, I guess? (laughs) So it was frustrating, it was, sometimes there was a point that I thought to myself I lost my identity.

Meanwhile, for Lucas, a 24-year-old recent university graduate, who grew up in the White-populated, medium-sized city of Kelowna and the more multiethnic city of Vancouver, geocultural contexts mattered in his identity work.

> When I go to Vancouver, because there are so many Asian Canadians, it's easy to say "I'm Canadian." (…) But in Kelowna, which is a very Caucasian-dominated city, it's hard to say I am Canadian, because in a small town like Kelowna, where the majority of people are Caucasian, I feel like I should look like them, and act like them… and the same lifestyle as them, like playing hockey and wearing a hockey jersey. So, it all depends on where I am. If I'm in Vancouver, I could say I'm Canadian, and I feel Canadian. If I'm in Kelowna, it's hard to say "I'm Canadian" because I'm not White. (…) We're definitely not White [like those] who claim they're Canadian. If we start to see more people who would look different, I think I would feel encouraged to call myself a Canadian as well.

Their family context is another important factor, as some interviewees had been deeply immersed in Korean media, culture, and language at home. Rosie, who grew up with parents who kept emphasizing her Korean identity, recalled how she was advised to identify her cultural identity.

> My parents were very strict on not speaking English in the house because they thought that they wanted me to be bilingual (…) In the past I felt like my identity was a 50/50 [i.e., 50% Canadian and 50% Korean]. (Laughs). It was actually what my parents were telling me to believe, but I am not actually feeling that way [i.e., I am more Canadian]. I don't think I could ever live there [i.e., Korea]. I never imagined myself living in Korea in the future.

The availability of ethnic options was believed by many of the interviewees. Apart from their experiences of being racialized and discriminated against, they also noted that their bicultural and bilingual attributes can be advantageous in certain circumstances. The young people who participated in interviews were able to speak Korean at least for conversational purposes, while primarily using English in their daily lives. "It's always an advantage for me to speak both languages," stated 24-year-old designer Stella from Vancouver. Ethan, a 28-year-old Toronto teacher also noted, "I know both cultures, so I'm almost like a hybrid, like blended in. So, more like open-minded." These accounts echo Kasinitz et al.'s (2008, p. 273) assertion of "the advantage of second generation immigrants," with which cultural differences are maintained or overcome.

However, these "advantages" may be questionable in reality. While most of the interviewees appreciated ethnic options and the potential of multicultural identities for Korean Canadians, a few remained critical about these "second generation advantages" (Kasinitz et al. 2008). For example, 23-year-old Henry in Toronto questioned the bicultural benefits of being Korean Canadians.

> Hyphen doesn't work, Korean-Canadian doesn't work, Canadian-Korean doesn't work. Korean who becomes Canadian doesn't necessarily work. Canadian who speaks Korean doesn't work. There are a lot of things that don't work in my experience.

While experiencing continued racialization and discrimination during their childhood, young Korean Canadians somehow explored their strategies to cope with pervasive racialization. Many seemed to be more accepting of their ethnic identity during late adolescence or during their university years. Some interviewees appreciated available ethnic options rather than simply seeking assimilation to the dominant "Canadian" culture. Speaking of their gradual acceptance of the Korean and Asian ethnic options, the young Korean Canadians in this book felt they became more "mature" (their own term) than before, while recalling their refusal to identify with their Korean origin as an "immature" state. In hindsight, several interviewees regretted having made an effort to quickly assimilate to the dominant cultural norms even at the expense of their culture and language. This "thinking of ethnicity" among second generation Koreans (D. Y. Kim 2013) has also been observed in several studies (D. Y. Kim 2013; Oh 2015). They gradually accepted their "second generation advantages" (Kasinitz et al. 2008) and believed that they had "more" ethnic options (which can potentially be transferrable to a form of cultural capital) compared to their White peers.

Imagination of Multicultural Canada

The young Korean Canadians' acceptance and affirmation of their ethnic identity especially in their late adolescence and youth seemed to be facilitated by their belief in the dominant multiculturalism ideology circulated widely in Canada through media and schooling. The young Korean Canadians commonly considered Canada as a multiculturalism-oriented country. For some interviewees, imagining Canada as a multicultural location appeared to be a strategy of negotiating racialization. While a dominant version of (liberal) multiculturalism might operate as an ideology that can serve to reproduce the existing cultural and racial order (Fleras 2014), the young people considered multiculturalism as a solution to or at least a refuge from existing racialization. Indeed, some interviewees emphasized Canada as a "culturally tolerant," "easy going" country, especially compared to the US or Korea. They identified multiculturalism as what distinguished Canada from other countries, such as the US. For Emily, a 25-year-old second generation Korean Canadian, Canada was a country that "embraces and retains traditions and cultures from other areas and respects them." She compared Canada with the US.

> If you look at the States [i.e., US], there are a lot of racist attacks. A lot of people that aren't afraid to show racism. But when you look at videos that were taken by other people on racial encounter in Canada, you always feel like bystanders standing up for the victim in Canada. But when you look at the States, no one says anything. (...) Canada is very multicultural. People respect that people can come from different countries. And they don't tolerate racism at all.

19-year-old Olivia similarly described Canada as "all encompassing" and a cultural mosaic.

> In Canada it's just really taboo if you don't accept anyone because of their culture. Because Canada is always all-encompassing. Is this, like a mosaic mentality, right? So it's "Oh, we're all Canadian." It's like, "we all love pancakes and maple syrup." (Laughs) So I really like that. It gives me a way to avoid the question of "Oh are you Chinese or are you Korean or are you something else?"

In the interviewees' accounts, while Korean culture was more concretely described, components of Canadian culture were not clearly identified especially among those who immigrated to Canada relatively late. For example, 19-year-old Olivia, who immigrated to Canada at the age of 9, pointed out, "One of the biggest problems with Canadian culture is that it doesn't exist." For some interviewees, Canada was considered as a country that has no culture, and thus, each ethnic group may claim their own cultural legacy. 16-year-old Sherry stated, "I feel like Canada doesn't really have a culture. In fact, I feel like it's just a culture that's made up of different cultures together because of how much diversity there is in the country. I would say that being Canadian is just being really nice." However, this description of Canada as an open and nice country of diversity may conceal the settler colonial history of the country in which Indigenous people and people of color have been severely oppressed.

Although most of the young Korean Canadians interviewed for this book had discriminatory experiences and felt marginalized, they at least partly celebrated their country of residence as a culturally diverse, inclusive country. The perception of Canada as a relatively open and inclusive country was evident among several interviewees who grew up in multi-ethnic neighborhoods in Toronto or Vancouver. However, according to several interviewees, openness may also mean emptiness of national symbols and cultural content. Many interviewees did not regularly access Canadian media content, such as the Canadian Broadcasting Corporation (CBC) programs, but rather frequently accessed American content through digital platforms such as Netflix. This finding resonates with critics' arguments that Canada lacks in national symbolic cultures and experiences, which may be related to the national mediascape where national content is assigned by regulation but remains unpopular among audiences (Taras 2015). According to Canadian media scholar Taras (2015), "Canada is the only developed country in the world whose citizens prefer watching foreign programming to watching domestically produced shows" (p. 207). Indeed, most of the interviewees were not very aware of popular Canadian media content and instead regularly viewed American shows. The near absence of experiences of regularly engaging with national cultural content was considered by the interviewees as an aspect of Canadian culture and the "multicultural" atmosphere of the country.

The young Korean Canadians' understanding of Canada as a multicultural country may reflect the publicly proposed ideology of liberal multiculturalism to some extent. As critics point out, the liberal or official version of multiculturalism implies a particular (hegemonic) way of managing difference (Fleras 2014; Henry and Tator 2010; Harris 2013). For example, as shown by the discourse of "cultural tolerance" adopted in the liberal multiculturalism framework, people of color and from immigrant backgrounds are defined as subjects "to be tolerated" by the dominant group of people (Brown 2006; Harris 2013). However, by appropriating the rhetoric of "multi-culture," the diasporic youth sought to reimagine their home country (Canada) as an open-ended location in which they can explore their own sense of belonging. In this regard, the diasporic youth's perception of Canada can be explained by the "new forms of national belonging" that Harris (2013) claimed in her study of migrant youth in Australia. Harris noted that many migrant youth refuse to participate in the imposed notion of the nation and national culture. Thus, according to her observations, "while many (young people) talked about the importance of feeling Australian, this was about acknowledgement of their equal belonging rather than a desire to embrace singular and exclusionary forms of national identification" (Harris 2013, p.134). The young Korean Canadians interviewed for this book may also challenge the top-down definition of Canada as a White-dominant nation-state, and seek their own imagination of Canada, in which their ethnic options and possible lives are realized.

ETHNIC IDENTIFICATION THROUGH HALLYU

The young Korean Canadians' experiences of racialization in their transition to adulthood taught them how to think about their ethnic identity and how to deal with the existing racial order. Most of the interviewees recalled that they felt ashamed about their difference as people of color, but gradually felt less shameful about who they were especially at university. In this process of exploring and reconnecting with ethnic identity, the recent Korean Wave phenomenon played a significant role. The rise of K-pop, Korean dramas (known as K-drama), and Korean films in the global mediascape contributed to motivating the diasporic youth to "come out" as ethnic subjects (Maira 2002). Furthermore, through Hallyu media, young Korean Canadians further explored and maintained their pan-Asian peer networks.

Mediated and Embodied Contact with Korea

Diasporic youth seek ethnic identity "because it provides a sense of community and self in the face of racial oppression" (Oh 2015, p. 5). Exploring ethnic identification and connecting with other Koreans—other 1.5 generation or second generation Korean Canadians, international Korean students, and Koreans in Korea—the diasporic youth in this book virtually or physically cross national borders and engage with their ancestral homeland. In this regard, the recent rise of transnational Hallyu through global digital media platforms allows the diasporic youth to access and reinterpret Koreanness. Recent Korean media's styles, themes, and content are considered highly hybrid and do not necessarily fit with the stereotypes of Korea, which the Western discourse of Orientalism conveniently assumes (Hong 2020). Diasporic youth's engagement with Hallyu offers *mediated* experiences of home-making, and it is sometimes synergized with *embodied* experiences of traveling to the ancestral home. That is, young Korean Canadians explore a sense of community by elaborating on their ethnic identification through several (often interwoven) activities, including mediated and embodied contact with their cultural heritage.

While mediated experiences with Hallyu media are increasingly significant for diasporic Korean youth, embodied contact with the ancestral homeland offers them intensive and impactful experiences, which trigger their interest in Korean language, culture, and Hallyu. Many young

Korean Canadians in this book recalled that their regular or occasional trips to Korea during childhood and adolescence enhanced their interest in Korea (Oh 2015, pp. 42–43). Except for one interviewee who was raised in the Greater Vancouver area and had never been to Korea, all the interviewed young people had been to Korea at least once at the time of interviewing. Some interviewees whose parents were relatively well off and had flexible work schedules spent several summer or winter breaks in Korea during their childhood, which contributed to reinforcing their ties with their ancestral homeland. Trips to the ancestral homeland seemed to play an overall positive role for the Korean Canadian youth in this book. A few interviewees who were enthusiastic about Hallyu used their trips to Korea as a form of pop culture pilgrimage. For example, second generation university student Paige, who is a K-pop fan, described a past trip to Seoul that occurred when she was in Grade 11.

> I was really into Korean media and K-pop and all that stuff. So the trip was really fun for me. So like visiting the labels like JYP, YG, and SM Entertainment companies [i.e., three major K-pop companies]. I went to their buildings and the concerts. So it was an overall very positive vacation.

Hallyu indeed influences how diasporic youth organize and make homecoming trips. They want to visit places they viewed on K-dramas and in K-pop music videos, and they want to do what Korean reality TV show participants do. For second generation Stella who has never been to Korea, a trip to Seoul is on her bucket list.

> Korean TV is just so interesting to me. It's just so fascinating to see what it looks like through Korean TV... like the food, the way they dress, subways, and getting a food delivery. It's just so interesting to me. So through TV I could learn what Koreans look like. If I go to Korea, I want to do so many things. Just anything like a normal Korean person would do. I wanna ride the subway, I wanna go to *hugeso* (a highway rest area), I wanna go to *sijang* (a traditional market)... All the stuff like that. Just like the daily things that Korean people do, but I never had the chance to.

In addition to and combined with homecoming trips, transnational Korean media was an essential resource for Korean Canadians to imagine their ancestral homeland. For example, 20-year-old Joanna noted, "Korean media is so important here in Canada. Koreans who grew up here don't know what is actually happening in Korea, and only know what they saw on TV. They think what TV says is true." 28-year-old schoolteacher Ethan, who was born in Canada, stated, "Watching Korean media makes me want to go to Korea more because it highlights the best parts in Korea." The interviewees were not all equally enthusiastic and excited about the Korean Wave, as a few interviewees did not extensively access Korean media in their daily lives. However, whether or not they were an enthusiastic consumers of Hallyu media, the Korean Canadians agreed that the Korean Wave can function as a form of "soft power" of Korea (Nye and Kim 2013), and eventually may contribute to enhancing the cultural recognition of diasporic Koreans.

Many interviewees appreciated the increasing availability of K-pop music videos and K-dramas on streaming platforms. Global circulation through digital media convergence has been considered a contributing factor in the rise of Hallyu (Jin 2016; S. Y. Kim 2018). Young people are introduced to K-pop or K-drama via digital platforms that synergistically connect different genres, content, and stars, while offering audiences transmedia experiences (S. Y. Kim 2018). 25-year-old Luke exemplifies how a Korean Canadian is introduced to Hallyu.

> I access it through the Internet because obviously I can't get Korean TV, news, or radio in Canada. You go on Internet websites. (…) You hear K-pop songs and, if you like it, you watch it, maybe a hundred times. And then you pirate it, or buy it. Mostly pirating I suppose. Yeah, so, that's how you get K-pop. And also YouTube, because most of it's video-based. So it's called video hopping, isn't it? You watch one, and you watch the next hundred, on the recommended. You also download TV shows. It's there. Sometimes you watch things like *Running Man*, [popular Korean entertainment TV show], you see pop stars, and obviously they're there to promote their new songs, so there's like a little clip of it. If you like it, go on YouTube, search up their name, right?

In this 2015 interview, Luke confirmed that "video hopping," followed by (pirate) downloading through commercial platforms or (illegal) streaming sites whose servers are overseas, is a popular way of accessing and consuming K-pop. Moreover, he implied different digital media are extensively used by both Hallyu industries and overseas audiences.

Most of the interviewees were initially exposed to Korean media through their parents when growing up. For many interviewees, their parents (first generation immigrants) were often depicted as someone who extensively consumed Korean media but rarely accessed non-Korean,

English media. 25-year-old Luke in Toronto, who immigrated at the age of 8, described his family home: "Inside my family's house is like little Korea. There's nothing very Canadian about it." 22-year-old Jim in Vancouver similarly stated, "I remember at our house we always had something playing on the TV and it was always Korean. My dad loved the reality TV shows and my mother loved dramas and would always just sit in front of the TV." Thus, it may be natural for young Korean Canadians to be familiar with Korean media from an early age. In some cases, Korean TV dramas offered time and space for family viewing. For example, 25-year-old Emily recalled that her family "usually watched a Korean drama everyday together."

The exposure to Korean media at home did not necessarily keep Korean Canadian youth interested in Korean media and popular culture. According to several interviewees, their early exposure to Korean media (via their parents during the pre- or early Hallyu period) did not always evolve into enthusiasm for more recent Hallyu media, such as K-pop (since the mid- or late 2010s), unless certain motivating factors were present. In some cases, early exposure even discouraged exploration of new Korean media. Several motivational factors, such as homecoming travel and friends' or family members' recommendations, were important in driving the young Korean Canadians' interest in Korean pop culture. Possessing the linguistic and cultural literacy necessary for understanding Korean media was another motivational factor in the diasporic young people's continued access to and interest in Korean media.

Although there was varied exposure, motivation, and interest related to Hallyu among the interviewees, the recent Hallyu media allowed the young Korean Canadians to access and reinterpret Koreanness and also feel positively attached to their ethnic roots. Thus, several 1.5 generation youth saw the rise of Hallyu as a badge of their ethnic pride. For example, 24-year-old Lucas, depicting himself as a K-pop "ambassador," noted that public interest in K-pop in North America is "a good thing" and he wanted to share his knowledge about Korea and K-pop further. Lucas, a fan of Blackpink, seemed to think that Korean fans were more authentic than other fans and he felt obliged to promote this Korean group whenever opportunities arose. For Lucas, consuming Hallyu media was to affirm his Korean ethnic identity and partly fulfill his cultural nostalgia through Korean language and imaginaries. In comparison, some other interviewees were somewhat reluctant to overtly promote Hallyu because they tried to avoid reducing their identities and cultural tastes to an ethnicity.

Overall, Hallyu is renewing diasporic young people's interest in their ethnic culture and identity (Oh 2015). For most of the interview participants, the Hallyu media significantly facilitated their interests in Korean culture and language as well as their ethnic identification. 21-year-old second generation Paige stated, "I had no knowledge of the Korean language until Grade 8 or 9. And then when I got into K-pop and K-drama that's where I basically re-learned Korean." In this manner, some second generation youth learned or were motivated to learn the Korean language out of their interest in K-pop, K-drama, or Korean entertainment shows. By consuming the imaginaries and representations of Korea, the diasporic youth were able to appreciate their own cultural heritages and come out as ethnic subjects.

Exploring Pan-Asian Ethnic Identity

As seen in the increasing multiethnic, global fandom of K-pop groups (e.g., Hong 2020; Jin et al. 2021), Hallyu media has been accepted and consumed by audiences with non-Korean backgrounds. Studies of Hallyu media have shown that diasporic Asian youth constitute a core overseas audience group of K-pop and K-drama (Ju and Lee 2015; McLaren and Jin 2020; Park 2013; Sung 2013; Yoon and Jin 2016). According to a recent survey of BTS fans in Canada, people of color (including those of Asian backgrounds) constituted over 60% of the survey respondents (McLaren and Jin 2020). Several empirical studies found that young audiences of Asian backgrounds identified with Hallyu media as a way of affirming their ethno-racial identities in response to White-dominant cultural contexts and media environments (T. S. Kim 2020; Sung 2013; Yoon 2017). According to Sung's (2013) study of Austrian youth of East Asian backgrounds, Hallyu media functions as a substitute for dominant Western media among the diasporic youth, while engagement with the Hallyu media becomes a significant marker of their self-identity. Moreover, Yoon's (2017) case study found that Asian Canadian youth's feelings of racial and cultural affinities with K-pop facilitated pan-ethnic consumption of Hallyu among diasporic youth. Similarly, Choi and Maliangkay (2015, p. 14) claimed that diasporic Asian fans consume K-pop as an ethno-cultural asset with self-celebratory fascination.

For fans of Asia and Asian diaspora/descent, the nature of this fascination is self-celebratory. For them it is a long-overdue vindication of their potency in cultural creativity. Summoning up an overinvested signifier of Asia, they would lay collective claim to K-pop and Hallyu as an embodiment of their ethno-cultural asset: "My cultures by my folks."

In this manner, Choi and Maliangkay (2015) suggested that Hallyu media served as cultural resources for young diasporic Asians' self-affirmation, which moves beyond the White-dominant cultural frame. The existing studies have described diasporic Asian youth as an important audience group in Hallyu. However, the studies focus on Asian youth of non-Korean backgrounds and thus have insufficiently examined how young people of Korean backgrounds and other Asian backgrounds interact with each other.

The diasporic youth interviewed for this book agreed that some of their Asian peers constitute the core fandom of K-pop and K-drama. According to the interviewees, some of their Asian Canadian friends are far more dedicated Hallyu fans. For example, Emily, a 25-year-old second generation Vancouverite who accessed Hallyu media but did not identify herself as a dedicated fan, spoke about her Hallyu-dedicated Asian friends.

I have a group of Asian friends who are very into K-pop and dancing and like celebrities and stuff. They are much more into K-pop than I am. They do like cover dance videos. They know all the celebrities by names. They go to their fan meetings stuff like that. I don't really talk to them about it because they're just on a different level.

Several interviewees identified cultural proximity as a key motivational factor in Asian Canadians' interest in Hallyu media. For example, 25-year-old Torontonian Luke observed that K-pop is an Asian youth cultural form, based on cultural proximities.

K-pop appeals more to Asian oriented people than non-Asians, to be explicit, White people, right? I think that's because first of all, proximity. And people are more used to it. (...) if you're Asian you're more likely to go seek out Asian food, Asian ethnic communities, and shopping malls, like Pacific Mall, right? So, it's like, if you go to those places, you're more likely to be exposed to Asian culture and content, including Korean. And then you, if you like it you get into, if you don't like it, you step out, right? So, non-Asians don't have that proximity and they're not likely to step into a Korean restaurant. I think that's the reason why it seems as if it's only Asian girls chasing an Asian pop star.

In this regard, it is not surprising that common interests in K-pop, K-drama, and Korean TV shows evolve among Asian Canadian youth. Several dedicated K-pop fans in this book were connected with their Asian peers in their fan activities. Especially in small fan group settings, they introduced K-pop content to their Korean Canadian and/or Asian Canadian peers. For example, 20-year-old Dale, who was a member of a dance group, recalled how his dance group turned to K-pop and K-pop cover dance.

> It got started when they actually were like listening to each other's songs. So one day I had my earphones on and the Taiwanese girl just took my earphones and started listening to it. And then she was like "Oh this is really catchy," and she started asking me "Is there a dance routine to this?" and I said "Yeah, there is." And then we first did our cover of a dance in the talent show, our school talent show. And that's how we actually got into it.

As Dale noted here, a cultural taste for K-pop was shared in intimate groups, comprised of primarily Asian Canadian young people. In such activities, transnational Korean media seemed to increasingly serve to facilitate inter-ethnic (pan-Asian) or intra-ethnic (between other diasporic Koreans) youth culture.

The dissemination of Hallyu between Asian Canadians reported by the interviewees shows how early trans-Asian flows of Hallyu in Asia may resurrect in North America and other non-Asian regions. Before its visible arrival in North America across the Pacific Ocean, Hallyu in the late 1990s and the early 2000s was known for its intra-Asian cultural flows, in which K-drama and K-pop created large fan bases in China, Japan, Taiwan, Singapore, and many other Asian locations (Chua and Iwabuchi 2008; Shin 2009). At least partly due to shared cultural and historical backgrounds, such as similar experiences of compressed, post-colonial modernization, Asian audiences were increasingly interested in Korean media, often as a supplement to or a substitute for Western media (Chua and Iwabuchi 2008). The intra-Asian cultural flows may be further diffused to diasporic Asians outside of Asia (Yoon and Jin 2016). Indeed, most of the interviewees agreed that K-pop and K-drama were common items through which they got along with their Asian Canadian peers.

As core consumers and early adopters, diasporic Koreans and Asians have played a pivotal role in the global rise of Hallyu (Park 2013). They are not only dedicated consumers but may also serve as "proselytizers" who adopt early and disseminate extensively Hallyu media. Jenkins et al. (2013) pointed out the role of diasporic audiences as "proselytizers" and disseminators of transnational cultural content. As discussed earlier, young Korean Canadians explore ethnic options by developing their attachments to being Korean, Asian, and Canadian, and they may share their cultural tastes with their peers of other Asian backgrounds.

Ambivalent Feelings About the Korean Wave

While increasing transnational flows of Korean media may facilitate young Korean Canadians' ethnic identification and positive self-affirmation, these young people do not always welcome this cultural trend. The diasporic young people interviewed for this book were sometimes worried about the racial and marginal meanings still attached to Korean media, which may reproduce Western stereotyping of Koreans and Asians. They also had ambivalent feelings about Western audiences' potential fetishization of Hallyu.

Stereotyping of the Korean Wave

The increasing publicity and popularity of K-pop and K-drama seemed to offer the Korean Canadians a cultural resource with which they felt positively about their ethnic identity and ties with Korea. However, Hallyu media has been racialized by general publics and mainstream media in Western contexts (Jin et al. 2021). Thus, the interviewees—especially those who participated in early interviews in 2015—expressed their concern about probable stigmatization and stereotyping by their (White) peers and the general public. In the interviewees' recollections, their cultural and ethnic connection with Korea used to be something they wanted to hide during their childhood and adolescence, but partly due to the recent wave of Hallyu, the young people seemed comfortable to now speak openly about their ethnic identity. Those interviewed in 2021 commonly noted that, perhaps due to extensive media coverage, Korean pop culture was sometimes mentioned in class or among peers.

For example, 16-year-old Kimberly was excited about the release of the McDonald's BTS meal in May 2021,[4] as many of her classmates were trying the menu item and taking a picture of it for their social media.

However, because Korean media is sometimes consumed and fetishized by Canadians of non-Korean backgrounds, the diasporic Korean youth had ambivalent feelings about the rise of Hallyu. Those who were interviewed in 2021 strongly agreed that Korean popular culture was consumed not only by ethnic Koreans but also increasingly by other young people. 16-year-old Samuel, who was interviewed in 2021, spoke about his surprise when he heard about BTS from his peers in school.

> In my school, my friends talk a lot about K-pop. There was a day they would be like, "Do you know who BTS is?" And I didn't even know who that was because when I was younger, I didn't really listen to any K-pop. And then I actually didn't know who this was. And after that, I went home and googled. And that's when I actually started listening to K-pop. Because my friend suggested it and I didn't want to be ashamed and embarrassed. So I started watching K-pop YouTube videos. And that's how I socialize with my friends these days.

This recent development was a surprise for the young Korean Canadians, especially when recalling their childhood during which they could not even speak Korean in front of their peers. Indeed, young Korean Canadians interviewed in an early phase of this book project (the mid-2010s) often noted the stigmatization of K-pop and K-pop fans. For example, 17-year-old Victoria, who grew up in predominately White-populated Kelowna, recalled in a 2015 interview her peers' reception of the "Gangnam Style" phenomenon that emerged a few years earlier: "At first, everyone thought he [Psy] was from North Korea, I was like, 'No! No!' They don't even know South and North Korea, so, I said, 'if you don't know North and South [Korea], don't say [he's from] North or South.'" 22-year-old Ava in Toronto described how the global hit of Psy's "Gangnam Style" made her "come out" as Korean in public places.

---

[4] Along with the release of BTS's new single "Butter" in Spring 2021, McDonald's launched a new combo item in 50 countries—the BTS-endorsed BTS meal. The meal's specifics had variations depending on the country, and thus, international fans shared pictures of BTS meals available in their neighborhood (Cannon 2021).

When Psy's "Gangnam Style" was in hype, I saw, not in Koreatown… it was around the Yonge and Eglinton area [a district in downtown Toronto]. I've seen Caucasian ladies just dancing and singing it. I've seen a lot of them. When I was just passing, people recognized that I was Korean, just random people would talk to me about "Gangnam Style" and stuff.

In most of the interviewees' recollections, due to such misrecognition and stereotyping of K-pop and other Korean media genres, cultural tastes for Hallyu often entailed stigmatization. Indeed, as empirical studies have shown, Hallyu and its fans have been racialized (Jung 2013; Won et al. 2020; Yoon 2019). Due to the White-dominant peer culture, some interviewees (especially those interviewed earlier in the mid-2010s) tried not to reveal their interest in Korean media when among their peers.

Circumstances have changed with the arrival of the recent phase of Hallyu, in which K-pop groups such as BTS have had record-breaking hits on major Western music charts and major Hallyu content and artists have attracted exceptional global attention in the late 2010s (see Chapter 1). However, whether positive or negative, the stereotyping of Korean media and its audiences appears to still remain. Henry, a 23-year-old 1.5 generation professional in Toronto, expressed his uncomfortable feelings about White people's assumptions about K-pop and Korean Canadians. "Caucasian people come up to me and say 'Oh, you're Korean! I love K-pop.' (…) It's like me going up to a White person and saying 'Oh, I love Coldplay. Your culture's so rich and beautiful. It's just the worst.'" In this manner, some interviewees refused to be identified with Hallyu media by others (especially White people) as they did not want to be pigeonholed only as an ethnic audience member naturally tied to Hallyu as a cultural trend that inevitably signifies its Korean origin.

Distancing from the Koreaboo

While Hallyu reaches to wider populations, beyond diasporic Asian youth, in Canada, the ways in which Korean pop cultural items are consumed in mainstream Western media and by White fans are not fully free of the Orientalist discourse of fetishizing and consuming the exotic other (Jin et al. 2021; Jung 2013). As addressed above, some Korean Canadian fans recognized the probable risk of cultural appropriation by White fans. Oh's (2017) analysis of White YouTubers' reaction videos on K-pop music showed that White audience members may assume a privileged position from which non-Western cultural forms are conveniently exploited to reproduce the existing racial order. However, given the recent development of K-pop fandom and its contribution to social justice campaigns since the late 2010s, the Orientalist gaze on the "K" in K-pop may be challenged by alternative voices with which this non-Western media genre is considered as "subcultural capital" (Thornton 1996) for imagining post-national and cosmopolitan worlds. K-pop may not be recognizable cultural capital among general publics and youth, but it may be increasingly adopted as a particular cultural currency among transnational subcultural groups and thus acquired (Jin et al. 2021).

While Hallyu has rapidly become a recognizable cultural genre among young people (including those of non-Korean or non-Asian background), this does not necessarily mean that the old Orientalist stereotyping of Asian culture no longer exists in Western audiences' consumption of Hallyu media. On the contrary, the stereotyping of K-pop has been reported in empirical studies (e.g., Min 2021; Yoon 2019). Stereotypes about Korean media are not only pervasive in mainstream media and audiences but also among fans of non-Korean backgrounds, who essentialize and romanticize Hallyu. In particular, some White fans of Hallyu media, including those who are often disapprovingly called "Koreaboo"[5] in K-pop fan communities and Western media, are considered by several interviewees as "weird," "immature," or "aggressive." 21-year-old K-pop fan Rebecca commented on extreme K-pop fans.

There's a new term coined for people who are overly obsessed with like Korean people, Koreaboos. It's gotten to the point where on YouTube or

---

[5] The Koreaboo usually means an obsessed non-Korean fan of Korea and Korean culture. It is believed that the term may have originated from a previously used term Weeaboo, referring to non-Japanese fans obsessed about Japanese culture (Won et al. 2020). Among Hallyu fans, the term has a very negative connotation as the Koreaboo is considered to fetishize not only their favorite Korean stars but the entire Korean culture and Koreans. Oli London, a British man in his early thirties, might be a widely known and extreme example of the Koreaboo. He underwent numerous plastic surgeries, which allegedly cost over USD100,000, to make his appearance look like a K-pop star. As a YouTuber and influencer, he even released the song and music video "Koreaboo" in 2021, which was temporarily listed on the iTunes K-pop chart. He has been a target of K-pop fans' harsh criticism because of his fetishization and misunderstanding of Korean culture and K-pop idols. Won et al. (2020) argued that the Koreaboo may be a discursive construction through which the dominant Western society marginalizes those who are fascinated about Asian culture.

on Facebook people are sharing cringy Koreaboo compilations. Sometimes you see that and I kind of wish that I wasn't associated with those people. (...) They're I guess ignorant towards the actual culture of Korea. Not just its pop culture. There's like a barrier between a real understanding of what Korea is all.

Kimberly, a 16-year-old high school student who grew up in the White-dominant city of Kelowna, was "the only Asian girl" in her school for a few years, and she critically noted the "fox-eye makeup fad" [i.e., a beauty trend that imitates the typical Asian eye shape through makeup and/or surgery] among White young women, which is undeniably influenced by the recent popularity of K-pop and other Asian stars.

They say it, in the media, "The Fox Eye." The eye shape. Even though they made fun of me for having that eye shape a while ago, but now that has become a trend. They all want that. Now a lot of girls are doing makeup to have their eyes to look more pointed as Asian eyes. They may follow the trend but they really don't know where it's from and they made fun of me for looking like that years ago, but now they wanna look like that. So I just think it's stupid of them.

Several interviewees noted that K-pop fans in their school excessively imitated their favorite K-pop idols' styles and fashion and thus circulated stereotypes of K-pop and its fans at school. That is, K-pop fans—especially those of non-Korean background—were described as (sometimes excessively) subcultural; those fans were described as being "weird," "unique," and "not popular." In response, some Korean Canadians who were frequent listeners or fans of K-pop tried to distance themselves from the Koreaboos in their schools (or in online forums). 18-year-old high school student Mia, who is herself a K-pop fan, spoke about the Koreaboo-type fans in her school and the online fan forums she often visited.

It's not like they do anything terrible but it's like an annoying thing, like they would constantly talk about it [K-pop] and quite a few of them actually went to school with a whole BTS outfit or something. I think that really makes them stand out and a target to everyone.

Mia and several other interviewees were critical of White K-pop fans who easily fantasize about Korea and Korean people. 16-year-old Kimberly also expressed a similar concern about Canadian K-pop fans of non-Korean backgrounds.

> They only see this shiny pop music side of Korea and they don't actually see the real culture and then they just fantasize about it. Some kids even want to become idols and they're not even Korean, and some people even fantasize about having a Korean or even Asian boyfriend, which I think is kind of terrible because something that is supposedly put out there for people to enjoy and respect all of their [idols'] hard work has been kind of turned into a fetish.

Due to the White fetishization of Korea observed among these K-pop fans, some young Korean Canadians expressed their mixed feelings about the rise of Hallyu in Canada and were hesitant in overtly exhibiting their cultural tastes for K-pop among their peers. While for Mia White K-pop fans were somewhat "embarrassing" and "annoying" in her own words, 19-year-old Cody considered their styles and attitudes as "weird" and "unique" (implying their subcultural nature).

> They are weird. That's not because they like K-pop. … They are really unique. How they wear, how they do their makeup. Unique people can't fit in to normal, regular, non-unique people, I think it's really hard to get in the (regular) community. So they try to find their way out of where they belong to.

In this manner, several interviewees who self-identified as K-pop fans distinguished themselves from White Koreaboo fans who seemed to have a "unique" subculture—a subculture that can engage with alternative cultural tastes but may not be free of existing stereotyping of Korean culture in a homogeneously and fetishized way, albeit positively. The Korean Canadians' concerns imply that Western K-pop fan culture can be dominated by these White Koreaboo fans and thus increase the risk of cultural appropriation and commodification of Korean culture. This book's findings resonate with those of recent studies that have examined how non-Korean or non-Asian fans of K-pop in North American, Europe, and Latin American contexts reproduce fetishism of Asian culture, which might be a new version of Orientalism (Hong 2013; Min 2021; Oh 2017).

According to the interviewees, the wave of Korean media seemed to contribute to enhancing cultural recognition of Korean and Asian

Canadians; however, the rapid rise of Hallyu that has interested many non-Korean fans may involve a risk of reproducing the Western gaze that essentializes and fetishizes Korean culture. As shown in some interviewees' criticism of White Koreaboo fans, diasporic young people's engagement with Hallyu involves certain ambivalent feelings. While acknowledging Hallyu media's role in facilitating ethnic identification for diasporic Koreans (to be further discussed in Chapter 3), the young Korean Canadians were also worried about Western appropriation of Korean media that may reproduce the Orientalist, Western gaze.

CONCLUSION

Diasporic Korean youth grow up realizing their difference, which adversely affects their self-identity and restricts their sense of belonging to the community. Their difference (and their own awareness of difference) limits the scope of their possible lives. As shown by numerous empirical studies conducted in North America, the racialization of people of color and immigrants systematically persists and restricts their career development on a social level (e.g., Oreopoulos 2011), while increasing their negative self-images as the other of "normal" Whites on a personal level (D. Y. Kim 2014). Growing up in "multicultural" Canada, young Korean Canadians go through moments of confusion and frustration owing to their difference. They feel that they are subject to (and have to be validated by) the dominant cultural norms of White Anglo groups, at least for a period in their childhood and/or adolescence. Yet, they gradually figure out how to negotiate the racial landscape to which they are forced to assimilate or otherwise remain stereotyped as the other. In doing so, they try to explore and negotiate their ethnic options and what it means to be Korean *and* Canadian (or to be in between Korean and Canadian), without necessarily sacrificing one for the other.

The recent global circulation of Korean media and popular culture may offer diasporic Korean youth resources for exploring who they are in between ethnic, Canadian, and multicultural identities. The increasing availability and recognition of Korean media in the global mediascape have allowed the diasporic Korean youth to openly engage with non-White Anglo cultural texts without self-monitoring or embarrassment. Young Korean Canadians are early adopters and reflexive consumers of the transnational cultural texts of Hallyu. Some engage with Hallyu as ethnic "ambassadors" who may have "authentic" feelings and knowledge about the texts, while others critically utilize the texts for reimagining their sense of belonging and bicultural or multicultural identities. Transnational cultural flows, such as Hallyu, offer a new cultural space in which diasporic youth can "maneuver at relative ease to create new opportunities for cultural production and expression" (Zhou and Lee 2004, p. 20). Transnational Korean media is utilized by diasporic Korean youth as a cultural resource for ethnic identification and connection. However, as addressed in this chapter, diasporic Korean Canadians also have ambivalent feelings about Hallyu, and with the recent global attention to Korean pop culture, some question the cultural appropriation of Hallyu by people of non-Korean backgrounds.

In the time of Hallyu, Korean Canadian entrepreneur Hanmin Yang's childhood identity question cited at the beginning of this chapter—"How do others see me?"(i.e., a question that implies visible minorities' precarious sense of identity in the White-dominant culture)—may be replaced with a more self-exploratory, self-assuring question for the forthcoming generations of diasporic youth in the time of the Korean Wave: "how do *we* see us through different lenses and different languages?"

References

BeyondAsian. 2020. Korean-Canadian builds Asian dating platform after devastating divorce. https://www.beyondasian.com/podcast/korean-canadian-builds-asian-dating-platform-after-devastating-divorce.

Bonilla-Silva, Eduardo. 2017. *Racism without racists: Color-blind racism and the persistence of racial inequality in the United States*, 5th ed. Lanham: Rowman & Littlefield.

Brown, Wendy. 2006. *Regulating aversion: Tolerance in the age of identity and empire*. Princeton: Princeton University Press.

Cannon, Matt. 2021. McDonald's BTS Meal is different depending where you buy it—Here's how. *Newsweek*, June 22. https://www.newsweek.com/mcdonalds-bts-meal-how-different-where-you-buy-1602631.

Choi, Jungbong, and Roald Maliangkay. 2015. Introduction: Why fandom matters to the international rise of K-pop. In *K-pop: The international rise of the Korean music industry*, ed. Jungbong Choi and Roald Maliangkay, 1–18. London: Routledge.

Chua, Beng Huat, and Koichi Iwabuchi, eds. 2008. *East Asian pop culture: Analysing the Korean Wave*. Hong Kong: Hong Kong University Press.

Danico, Mary Yu. 2004. *The 1.5 Generation: Becoming Korean American in Hawaii*. Honolulu: University of Hawaii Press.

Fleras, Augie. 2014. *Racisms in a multicultural Canada: Paradoxes, politics, and resistance*. Waterloo: Wilfrid Laurier University Press.

Ghosh, Ratna. 2008. Racism: A hidden curriculum. *Education Canada* 48 (4): 26–29.

Harris, Anita. 2013. *Young people and everyday multiculturalism*. London: Routledge.

Henry, Frances, and Carol Tator. 2010. *The colour of democracy: Racism in Canadian society*, 4th ed. Toronto: Nelson Education.

Hong, Seok-Kyeong. 2013. *Hallyu in globalization and digital culture era: Full House, Gangnam Style, and after*. Paju: Hanul Academy [in Korean].

Hong, Seok-Kyeong. 2020. *BTS: On the road*. Seoul: Across [in Korean].

Hovey, Joseph D., Sheena E. Kim, and Laura D. Seligman. 2006. The influences of cultural values, ethnic identity, and language use on the mental health of Korean American college students. *The Journal of Psychology* 140 (5): 499–511.

Jenkins, Henry, Sam Ford, and Joshua Green. 2013. *Spreadable media: Creating value and meaning in a networked culture*. New York: New York University Press.

Jin, Dal Yong. 2016. *New Korean Wave: Transnational cultural power in the age of social media*. Champaign: University of Illinois Press.

Jin, Dal Yong, Kyong Yoon, and Wonjung Min. 2021. *Transnational Hallyu: The globalization of Korean digital and popular culture*. Lanham: Rowman & Littlefield.

Joshee, Reva. 2004. Citizenship and multicultural education in Canada: From assimilation to social cohesion. In *Diversity and citizenship education: Global perspectives*, ed. James A. Banks, 127–156. San Francisco: Jossey-Bass.

Ju, Hyejung, and Soobum Lee. 2015. The Korean Wave and Asian Americans: The ethnic meanings of transnational Korean pop culture in the USA. *Continuum: Journal of Media and Cultural Studies* 29 (3): 323–338.

Jung, Eun-Young. 2013. K-pop female idols in the West. In *The Korean Wave: Korean media go global*, ed. Youna Kim, 106–119. London: Routledge.

Kasinitz, Philip, John H. Mollenkopf, Mary C. Waters, and Jennifer Holdaway. 2008. *Inheriting the city: The children of immigrants come of age*. New York: Russell Sage Foundation.

Kibria, Nazli. 2002. *Becoming Asian American: Second-generation Chinese and Korean American identities*. Baltimore: John Hopkins University Press.

Kim, Dae Young. 2013. *Second-generation Korean Americans: The struggle for full inclusion*. El Paso: LFB Scholarly Publishing LLC.

Kim, Dae Young. 2014. Coping with racialization: Second-generation Korean-American responses to racial othering. *Second-generation Korean experiences in the United States and Canada*, ed. Pyong Gap Min and Samuel Noh, 145–165. Lanham: Lexington Books.

Kim, Nadia Y. 2018. Race-ing the Korean American experience. In *A companion to Korean American studies*, ed. Rchael Miyung Joo and Shelley Sang-Hee Lee, 267–303. Leiden: Brill.

Kim, Suk-Young. 2018. *K-pop live: Fans, idols, and multimedia performance.* Stanford: Stanford University Press.

Kim, Tae-Sik. 2020. Young migrant Vietnamese in the Czech Republic reflect diasporic contexts in their identification of cultural proximity with Korean media. *Journal of Intercultural Studies* 41 (4): 524–539.

Kim, Il-Ho, Neha Ahmed, and Samuel Noh. 2014. Perceived discrimination and mental health in Korean-Canadian youth: Salience of ethnic pride as a moderator. In *Second-generation Korean experiences in the United States and Canada*, ed. Pyong Gap Min and Samuel Noh, 125–143. Lanham: Lexington Books.

Lewis, Amanda E. 2004. "What group?" Studying whites and whiteness in the era of "color-blindness." *Sociological Theory* 22 (4): 623–646.

Maira, Sunaina. 2002. *Desis in the House: Indian American youth culture in New York City.* Philadelphia: Temple University Press.

McLaren, Courtney, and Dal Yong Jin. 2020. "You can't help but love them": BTS, transcultural fandom, and affective identities. *Korea Journal* 60 (1): 100–127.

Min, Wonjung. 2021. Mis Chinos, Tus Chinos: The Orientalism of Chilean K-pop fans. *International Communication Gazette* 83 (8): 799–817.

Moodley, Kogila. 1998. Antiracist education through political literacy: The case of Canada. In *Critical multiculturalism*, ed. Stephen May, 159–175. London: Routledge.

Nye, Joseph, and Youna Kim. 2013. Soft power and the Korean Wave. In *The Korean Wave: Korean media go global*, ed. Youna Kim, 31–42. London: Routledge.

Oh, David C. 2015. *Second-generation Korean Americans and transnational media: Diasporic identifications.* Lanham: Lexington Books.

Oh, David C. 2017. K-pop fans react: Hybridity and the white celebrity-fan on YouTube. *International Journal of Communication* 11: 2270–2287.

Oreopoulos, Philip. 2011. Why do skilled immigrants struggle in the labor market? A field experiment with thirteen thousand resumes. *American Economic Journal: Economic Policy* 3 (4): 148–171.

Park, Jung-Sun. 2013. Negotiating identity and power in transnational cultural consumption. In *The Korean Wave: Korean media go global*, ed. Youna Kim, 120–134. London: Routledge.

Seol, Kyoung Ok, Hyung Chol Yoo, Richard M. Lee, Ji Eun Park, and Yena Kyeong. 2016. Racial and ethnic socialization as moderators of racial discrimination and school adjustment of adopted and nonadopted Korean American adolescents. *Journal of Counseling Psychology* 63 (3): 294–306.

Shin, Hyunjoon. 2009. Have you ever seen the Rain? And who'll stop the Rain?: The globalizing project of Korean pop (K-pop). *Inter-Asia Cultural Studies* 10 (4): 507–523.

Song, Miri. 2003. *Choosing ethnic identity*. Oxford: Polity.

Sung, Sang-Yeon. 2013. Digitization and online cultures of the Korean Wave. In *The Korean Wave: Korean media go global*, ed. Youna Kim, 135–147. London: Routledge.

Taras, David. 2015. *Digital mosaic: Media, power, and identity in Canada*. Toronto: University of Toronto Press.

Thornton, Sarah. 1996. *Club cultures: Music, media, and subcultural capital*. Middletown: Wesleyan University Press.

Tuan, Mia. 1998. *Forever foreigners or honorary Whites? The Asian ethnic experience today*. New Brunswick: Rutgers University Press.

White, Shelley. 2011. School lunches: Is your child a victim of lunchbox bullying? *Huffington Post Canada*, September 1. https://www.huffingto npost.ca/2011/09/01/school-lunch-bullying_n_944609.html.

Won, Yong-Jin, Huikyong Pang, Jun-hyung Lee, and Marisa Luckie. 2020. Koreaboo, a missing piece of the BTS universe puzzle. *Korean Journal of Journalism & Communication Studies* 64 (4): 471–499 [in Korean].

Yoon, Kyong. 2017. Cultural translation of K-pop among Asian Canadian fans. *International Journal of Communication* 11: 2350–2366.

Yoon, Kyong. 2019. Transnational fandom in the making: K-pop fans in Vancouver. *International Communication Gazette* 81 (2): 176–192.

Yoon, Kyong, and Dal Yong Jin. 2016. The Korean Wave phenomenon in Asian diasporas in Canada. *Journal of Intercultural Studies* 37 (1): 69–83.

Zhou, Min. 2004. Are Asian Americans becoming "White?" *Contexts* 3 (1): 29–37.

Zhou, Min, and Jennifer Lee. 2004. Introduction: The making of culture, identity, and ethnicity among Asian American youth. In *Asian American youth: Culture, identity, and ethnicity*, ed. Jennifer Lee and Min Zhou, 1–30. London: Routledge.

CHAPTER 3

Diasporic Viewing of Korean TV

Abstract The young Korean Canadians' diasporic viewing of Korean TV reveals how Hallyu media is integrated into viewers' everyday contexts. In the midst of White-dominant media representation, the increasing global popularity of Korean TV may provide the diasporic youth with an option for exploring how they can critically navigate between different cultural texts and contexts. Narrative Hallyu media and its storytelling allow the young people to identify themselves with the distant (ancestral) homeland and furthermore to engage with non-Western storytelling and representation without self-monitoring and feelings of marginalization.

Keywords Hallyu (The Korean Wave) · Diasporic youth · Diasporic TV · Korean TV · K-drama · Digital platform · Participatory culture · Personal broadcasting · Vlogging · Paratext

In a Canadian radio interview (Q on CBC 2018), the Korean American actor Steven Yeun, who spent a part of his early childhood in the Canadian city of Regina before settling in the US, spoke about his experience filming the Korean film *Burning* (2018). Yeun stated that, while filming, he was able to find a side of himself that he did not see before. He described the experience of playing a Korean character in the Korean film produced with a Korean crew. Reflecting on his usual American film projects, in which performing an *Asian* character rather than a character

K. Yoon, *Diasporic Hallyu*, East Asian Popular Culture,
https://doi.org/10.1007/978-3-030-94964-8_3

was implicitly incorporated into his roles (whatever the role), Yeun said, "When in Korea they don't think about that. They just go that's 'You are that character now.'" Then, he added with a glimpse of a smile on his face, "You feel what you can't explain here. (Interviewer: Tell me more about it) You know what it is? It's that the gaze and the lens of the Western world is not upon you anymore. So you don't have to explain yourself. You can just be. I think that's the key distinction."

Yeun's experience echoes young Korean Canadians' experiences of racialization during their growing up in Canada. As addressed in the previous chapter, the diasporic youth were often aware of the Western and White gaze and felt marginalized. By internalizing the White-dominant cultural frame, they learned to see themselves as ethnic or racial subjects, rather than seeing themselves from their own perspective. In this regard, Korean Wave (or Hallyu) media seems to offer new cultural resources with which the diasporic Korean youth can see themselves without referring to, and being validated by, the White gaze.[1]

The pressure to internalize the White-dominant cultural frame is exercised through various everyday contexts. Media plays a crucial role in shaping and maintaining the hegemonic discourse of Whiteness-as-a norm (Dyer 1997). The near absence of Korean or Asian characters and themes in the Canadian mediascape (Fleras 2011) may reinforce the diasporic youth's compliance to the White gaze. Grace, a 19-year-old student who grew up in Vancouver, only recently began to question why there were no Asians on Canadian TV.

> When I was younger, I watched Canadian shows on the Family Channel. I didn't see many Asians. I saw Latino and Black people but no Asians.

---

[1] According to Korean acafans' (academics who are also fans) research monographs on the K-pop group BTS and its fandom (Hong 2020; J. Lee 2019), one of the reasons that BTS has gained momentum to attract young people's support across the globe may be the group's promotion that does not rely on Western market standards. In particular, while the group's latest songs are written in English, BTS was not desperate to sing in English to penetrate Western markets but continued to sing in Korean at least for its formative period, and in so doing expressed their own experiences and feelings more effectively. Such an approach encouraged global fans to make an effort for, and participate in, cultural translation from their own perspective. This room for translation and participation has substantially distinguished BTS from Western musicians. Moreover, BTS's music has delivered a message of "Be Yourself" and "Love Yourself" mostly in the Korean language without necessarily complying to Western codes and values. Their music may offer many people of color the freedom to be themselves in their own language.

So I felt that I was underrepresented. But I didn't really notice it. I didn't really notice it until people have told me about the issue. (…) I felt it was normal, but it wasn't. I felt like it was normal that Asian people weren't on TV shows because it is Canada. It wasn't until I was older that I thought like "Oh, maybe it's good to have an Asian in TV shows as well because my friends are all Asians."

In Grace's account, the clause "because it is Canada" may reveal how she learned to think about the ethno-racial composition and diversity of Canada. Grace, who immigrated at the age of 6 and grew up in Vancouver, might have been instructed to believe that Canada was represented primarily by White people but not by any people of color.[2]

The absence of representation or the misrepresentation of Korean and Asian people on Canadian TV may function to justify the White-dominant cultural frame that maintains and reinforces "the gaze and the lens of the Western world" pointed out by Steven Yeun. The stereotypes of Asians in North America, which emerged as early as the eighteenth century, have reduced Asians as the "yellow peril" who are dishonest, uncivilized, and inferior to Whites and thus considered to be a great threat to Whites (Lyman 2000). In comparison, a relatively recent (since the 1960s) Western stereotype of Asians is the model minority trope that essentializes Asian culture to explain Asian Americans' relatively successful upward social mobility; this seemingly positive stereotype in practice serves to "construct Asians as immutably foreign and unassimilable with whites"

---

[2] Grace's thoughts are not surprising given that Canadian media and public discourses have drawn on the White dominant cultural frame in which White people are represented as the norm. Among others, one recent example that illustrates the White dominant cultural frame and representation is the 100 dollar bill controversy in 2011. As a routine renewal process, the Bank of Canada launched new banknotes in 2011. In this round of renewal, the Bank considered the image of an Asian-looking female scientist on the new 100 dollar bills. However, after receiving complaints from a few members in focus groups that were conducted for early consultation in Calgary, Toronto, Montreal, and Fredericton, the Bank decided to remove the Asian-looking character to replace it with a character with "neutral ethnicity." Reportedly, one focus group member commented, "The person on it appears to be of Asian descent which doesn't rep(resent) Canada. It is fairly ugly." After the controversy, the Bank released the official 100 dollar bills with a character who appears to be Caucasian. The replacement was harshly criticized by Asian Canadians and their associations (Canadian Press 2012). This example shows how Asian Canadians have been marginalized in, and almost erased from, the country's public imagination; Asian Canadians have often been invisible and treated as not being eligible to represent Canada (C. Kim 2016).

(Li and Nicholson 2021, p. 4). The model minority stereotype also serves to maintain the ideology of White privilege as it "helps to divide racial minority groups by pitting Asians and other minorities against each other and leads to discounting structural and cumulative disadvantages that other minority communities face" (Li and Nicholson 2021, p. 4).

Most of the young Korean Canadians interviewed for this book experienced racialization as they were marginalized by the yellow peril trope in which Asians' behaviors, appearances, and foods are "not as normal as" Whites; otherwise (especially in relatively Asian-populated locations), they were pigeonholed as those who were docile and only good at study (but not at other activities) according to the model minority trope. While growing up, the young Korean Canadians (like many other Asian Canadians) were forced to conform to these two dominant stereotypes of Asians. They learned to see themselves as the other of the dominant group. In this regard, Hallyu appears to be a significant moment in which Korean and other Asian diasporic youth explore ways to see themselves without referring to the White gaze.

This chapter examines how young Korean Canadians engage with narrative-based Hallyu genres (dramas, entertainment shows, films, and vlogs), which will also be referred to as "Korean TV" as a whole. The Korean TV in this chapter does not narrowly refer to programs that are broadcast via network TV channels but includes a wide range of narrative content transmitted via digital screens; other newer media practices, such as personal vlogs (e.g., live streaming eating shows), and Korea-themed overseas media (e.g., the Canadian Broadcasting Corporation's *Kim's Convenience*) are also examined.

This chapter focuses on narrative media genres to address how diasporic youth engage with transnational Korean media as they navigate between the media of "here" (the country of residence) and "there" (the ancestral homeland) while seeking to feel at home. In so doing, the chapter discusses how diasporic young people explore new modes of representation, which move beyond the White-dominant mediascape of Canada. The study of diasporic young people's reception of transnational Korean TV suggests that narrative genres contribute to young Korean Canadians' engagement with their ancestral homeland and ethnic identity as well as their diasporic "feeling at home" in their everyday contexts (Brah 1996). Furthermore, by engaging with Korean TV, the diasporic youth may explore how they can see themselves not necessarily through the Western gaze but through bicultural navigations.

KOREAN TV IN NORTH AMERICA

Beginning of Hallyu Through Korean TV

While K-pop has increasingly received global media attention owing to a series of mega hits by the K-pop group BTS, Korean narrative media genres have also been globally disseminated for decades. In fact, looking back at the history of Hallyu, made-in-Korea TV dramas, entertainment shows, and films played a significant role in the beginning of the wave in the late 1990s and early 2000s. In particular, several intra-Asian hit dramas, including the romantic drama *Winter Sonata* (2002) and the historical drama *Dae Jang Geum–Jewel in the Palace* (2003), initiated the early surge of Hallyu in a wide range of Asian countries, popularizing the phrase "the Korean Wave" (Hallyu). Thus, early Hallyu studies focused on drama audiences and industries (e.g., Chua and Iwabuchi 2008), whereas scholarly attention has shifted to K-pop in the later phase (e.g., Choi and Maliangkay 2015; Fuhr 2016). The popularity of Korean dramas (known as K-drama) has been globally expanded further in collaboration with global streaming sites, including Netflix, through which many K-dramas have gained global viewership, for example *Descendants of the Sun* (2016) and *Crash Landing on You* (2019). As of 2020, dramas are the most popular Hallyu genre for overseas consumers (Korea Foundation for International Cultural Exchange 2021). While K-drama has been acclaimed for its high production values and growing audience bases (Ju 2021), some of the genre's conventions, such as the excessive use of clichés and the patriarchal portrayal of women, have been criticized (An 2022).

Korean TV has attracted intra-Asian and global audiences owing to several factors such as cultural proximities (especially among Asian audiences in Asia or diasporic contexts) and relatable experiences of modernity projected in K-dramas (Chua and Iwabuchi 2008; Han 2019; T. S. Kim 2020). More specifically, emotional engagement through romantic comedies and melodramas has been identified as a key factor in K-drama's growing global fan bases (Ju 2020). According to Ju's (2020) study, US audiences express their "desire to relax, seek comfort, and find entertainment in these dramas" and find "emotional attachment to the K-drama narrative" (45). Kim and Li (2018) found that Korean entertainment game shows are particularly appealing to Asian audiences with their harmonious, family-like interactions between celebrity hosts and guests, without promoting individualized competition. Shared Asian experiences of rapid modernization may be another component with which the Asian audiences can identify. That is, Hallyu media has been recognized as cultural content symbolizing the most advanced Asian form of modernization and has arguably emerged as "the new Asian hegemony" (Leung 2021, p. 192).

Asian audiences' viewing positions may be further compared with people of Asian heritage who reside outside of Asia. That is, diasporic Asian audiences are attracted to Korean TV as they identify with particular values portrayed in the dramas, such as family norms and work ethics (T. S. Kim 2020). In addition to K-dramas, Korean entertainment shows (*yeneung*), such as *Running Man* (2010–present) and *Infinite Challenge* (2005–2013), have been popular among young people. Popular Korean entertainment shows have been introduced to overseas audiences through local remakes. The exportation of TV formats (not the exportation of final content products) has been a new component of Hallyu. For example, *Running Man* has been localized and remade as the Chinese show *Hurry Up, Brother* (2014–present), which was also followed by its Vietnamese version (2019–present). Among increasing format exports in the Hallyu industries, *King of Mask Singer* (*Bongmyeongawang*, 2015–present)[3] is especially noteworthy as the show's format was sold globally, while being acclaimed as "a game changer in global TV" (R. Wang 2019). These comical game shows, which sometimes include guest appearances by K-pop idols and/or other Hallyu celebrities, have been especially appealing to young audiences (Kim and Li 2018).

Digital Platforms

Korean TV's increasing popularity was not only driven by its content, themes, and formats, but also its digital platforms (i.e., the ways the content is delivered). Many of the Korean Canadians interviewed for this book were heavily reliant on the Internet through mobile devices and thus appreciated the importance of the digital circulation of Hallyu media. In her interview in 2015, 22-year-old Emma praised Korean TV's intimate

---

[3] *King of Mask Singer* (produced by Munhwa Broadcasting Corporation) is a singing competition and guessing game show in which celebrity participants wear a mask to hide their identity and compete with each other by singing. The show's format has been sold to over 50 countries and developed as *The Masked Singer* franchise (Middleton 2020).

and relevant content, and she appreciated the role of the Internet that allows her to gain knowledge about her ethnic homeland.

> It's like "Oh, thank goodness!" I can watch Korean TV here. Before over 5 years ago, we didn't have an immediate access right? When there is a show comes up in Korea, you get it next day. I think it's a fortunate thing to get it really quickly here.

Illegal downloading was a method for prompt access to an extensive range of Hallyu media among the earlier 2015 interviewees, but most of the interviewees seemed to primarily use streaming services, including Netflix, Viki, and YouTube. Owing to the Hallyu industries' diligent integration into global digital platforms, as well as the fans' voluntary contributions through their translation labor, a large number of Korean films and TV shows have become available on global digital platforms, such as Netflix, and some shows have been acclaimed by both global viewers and critics. Moreover, Korean directors and producers have increasingly collaborated with Netflix to create Netflix original content, such as *Okja* (2017) and *Kingdom* (2019–2021). Dramas, entertainment shows, and films have certainly been an integral component of the rapidly rising Hallyu, and global streaming platforms (also known as OTT, or Over-The-Top services) have paid particular attention to Hallyu content. Korean TV programs have increasingly been streamed through global OTT services, whereas an increasing number of shows have been funded by, or have collaborated with, overseas media corporations. Netflix announced its plan to invest 500 million dollars in 2021 alone to add more Korean media content to its repertoire (M. Kim 2021). The Hallyu industries' collaboration with Netflix has often been considered as an opportunity for the global dissemination of Hallyu content (Ju 2021), and Netflix's incorporation of Korean content has also contributed to the company's growing market share in the Korean OTT market. Owing to its aggressive investment in Korean content and streaming service booms during the pandemic, Netflix rapidly emerged as the dominant player (40% share of the Korean OTT market, which is far higher than any other service providers) in Korea—the birthplace of Hallyu—and is considered as a threat to domestic OTT businesses (Kwon 2021).

In terms of the dollar amount of exported Korean TV dramas, for the entire overseas export in 2018, Asia was the largest market of Hallyu TV (65.5%) followed by North America (21.4%); Japan, the US, Taiwan,

China, and Hong Kong were also large market countries (Noh 2020).[4] North America has been a main overseas market for Korean TV even before the recent wave of Hallyu. Korean diasporas in the US and Canada have constituted a loyal audience group (Park 2013). In Canada, the Korean language speciality channel *All TV* was established in 2001 and has offered licensed Korean network TV programs as well as its own Canada-produced programs. *All TV* is packaged into major Canadian digital TV service providers (e.g., Bell and Rogers), and several interviewees' families subscribed to this service. However, most of the young people interviewed for this book accessed Korean TV online via illegal or licensed streaming sites, such as YouTube and Netflix. A few participants interviewed earlier in 2015 accessed Korean TV by (illegally) downloading on their laptop computers and sharing the files with their peers or by viewing through illegal streaming sites, but this tendency appeared to be replaced with viewing through subscription-based streaming sites (e.g., Netflix and Viki). It was noticed in the later interviews that the young people also navigated to watch clips of Korean TV available on YouTube through their mobile phones in between their daily routines.

Streaming Korean TV

Most of the young people in this book were using (legal or illegal) video steaming sites to access Korean TV. As demonstrated by several studies, diasporic Koreans were early promoters of Korean TV in North America and elsewhere (S. Lee 2015; Park 2013; Yoon 2020). Early video streaming services that emerged in the US were indebted to diasporic Korean fans' labor and creativity, and these streaming services contributed to expanding North American (and global) audience bases of K-dramas.

---

[4] Until 2016, Japan and China were the two largest overseas Korean TV drama markets, which constituted over 50% of all K-drama exports. However, the exportation of Korean TV dramas to China rapidly decreased after 2016 due to the Chinese government's severe control of Korean media imports. China's ban on Korean media and cultural content was in response to the 2016 South Korea-US agreement on the launch of the US Terminal High Altitude Area Defense (THAAD) system in Korea, which the Chinese government claimed could potentially be used to spy into Chinese territory. In protest, China restricted the importation of Hallyu content to a large extent and this ban by and large continues as of 2021. Because China has been a major overseas market for the whole Hallyu industry, this "Anti-Korean Wave" policy negatively impacted the Hallyu industries (i.e., a significant decrease in international trade profits) (Frater 2021; Jun 2017).

For example, Viki, a popular US-grown video streaming site (currently owned by Japanese media corporation Ratuken) that began to stream many K-dramas prior to Netflix, was founded in 2007 by three young entrepreneurs, including two Korean Americans (Changseong Ho and Jiwon Moon). This streaming service initially relied on collaborative fan-based translations and subtitles for the prompt circulation of K-dramas in overseas contexts. In the early phase of this service, bilingual fans who speak Korean and English collaboratively and voluntarily provided their fan labor for subtitles that have contributed to boosting the global viewership of K-drama (Dwyer 2017; Henthorn 2019). The video streaming site DramaFever (2009–2018) is another example of a Korean American-led venture business that contributed to expanding global audience bases for Korean media. Established by two Korean Americans (Seung Bak and Suk Park), DramaFever was an early, legitimate streaming site for Korean TV content in the US, and the two Korean American founders aimed to "turn the existing illegal services into legitimate ones" (S. Lee 2015, p. 182). After its growth, this popular site was acquired by the media conglomerate Warner Bros. and later discontinued due to "business reasons" (Spangler 2018).

Several early streaming services, such as Viki and DramaFever, demonstrate how diasporic Koreans in North America have contributed to the rise of Hallyu as early adopters, audiences, and/or venture entrepreneurs. In particular, bilingual youth who speak English and Korean have facilitated a unique fansubbing culture, in which grassroots translations are offered, shared, and revised before the official translations (by the distributors) are created. Viki and DramaFever are known for their extensive use of volunteer fan translators' labor (S. Lee 2015). Along with a unique fansubbing culture, North American fans of Korean heritage have developed a mode of communal watching through digital platforms such as Viki, which allow real-time comments on the shows (Dwyer 2017).[5]

---

[5] These streaming sites emerged prior to the global domination of major streaming services (e.g., Netflix) and played an important role in introducing overseas Hallyu audiences to licensed content markets. Global K-drama viewers who had to be reliant on piracy due to the lack of properly licensed and translated content gradually transited to established streaming services. The histories of these Korean American-launched streaming sites illustrate how venture business inspired by media fan practices is later purchased by media conglomerates (Viki by Ratuken and DramaFever by Warner Bros.) and thus commodifies fans' insider knowledge and skills (such as interactive translation and commenting) (Jin et al. 2021).

Given that K-pop fans also extensively engage in the creation and sharing of paratexts associated with the original texts (Cruz et al. 2021), diasporic Korean youth—especially those who contribute to subtitling or other paratext practices—play a pivotal role in the translation and dissemination of Hallyu.

BEING HERE AND THERE THROUGH KOREA TV

Due to their storytelling associated with (ancestral) homelands, narrative genres—drama, films, and entertainment shows—constitute an important component of everyday life in diasporas (Aksoy and Robins 2000; Gillespie 1995). Korean TV allows the diasporic Korean youth to immerse themselves in their imaginary and ethnic homeland through engaging narratives that combine intimate feelings and (physically) distant locations. Via the Internet, the young Korean Canadians navigate transnational Korean TV, along with Anglophone (mostly American and partly Canadian) TV. The regular (if not frequent) exposure to Korean TV facilitates their reimagination of Korea as an intimate destination with which they can identify.

Navigating with the Wave

Some interviewees omnivorously watched what was available and appealing to them on streaming services, whereas a few others watched far more Korean TV than American and Canadian. Interestingly, compared to American and Korean TV content, that of Canadian TV was far less consumed. 22-year-old Emma in Toronto said, "I don't really watch shows and dramas that are Canadian. Canadian shows are not popular." This response was echoed by many other interviewees who did not consciously access Canadian TV and thus did not make a clear distinction between American and Canadian TV. In particular, when asked about Canadian TV viewing, a common response was that of Kevin, a 22-year-old student in Toronto, who regularly watched American and Korean TV shows: "Um… Canadian… I don't have access to cable. So, I can't watch TV. Well, I don't actually watch Canadian TV." 21-year-old student Julia noted, "I think just non-Canadian programs [referring to American shows] are more accessible because I am on Netflix and stuff." The interviewees were more likely to be on streaming sites, such as Netflix, rather than accessing Canadian TV channels, such as the Canadian Broadcasting Corporation (CBC).

Among the abundant media content increasingly available through digital platforms, the interviewees engaged with transnational Korean media in their pursuit of ethnic identification and navigation between here and there. For second generation Vivian, a 23-year-old student in Toronto who had not visited Korea in 10 years, Korean TV was an important means to feel and learn about her ancestral homeland.

> Watching Korean TV through the Internet helped me integrate with Korea more as I was in Canada all my life. I did use the Internet a lot to connect with Korean society. By watching Korean dramas, I realize, "Oh, this is the fashion trend in Korea," or I learn how people think and what their values are in Korea. By watching Korean dramas, you can tell Koreans are very hard working and their culture is nice. The good part of Korean culture made me proud of who I am. By seeing Korean society through the Internet, I felt I didn't wanna give up being Korean. That's why I stopped from becoming more than 50% Canadian. In a sense, it kind of stopped me becoming fully Canadian.

For Vivian, keeping the Korean side of her identity became increasingly important as she grew older and, in this process, Korean TV played an integral role.

Many interviewees had been exposed to Korean TV while growing up. Owing to their parents who viewed Korean TV via DVDs, streaming sites, or digital TV packages, Korean TV was considered by most of the interviewees as a kind of background music in their family home. By viewing K-dramas, the young people improved or kept up with their Korean speaking/listening skills and remained informed about contemporary Korea. By doing so, they maintained their sense of being connected to Korea. For example, Julia, a 21-year-old student who immigrated at the age of 6, watched both English language TV and Korean TV. She tried to consciously watch Korean TV as a method of maintaining her ethnic identity.

> What I like about English-based TV programs is that I can understand 100% of what they are saying. But 85% of Korean TV. Yeah, there are sometimes things that I don't understand [in Korean TV]. I tried to figure out what they are saying. (…) If I didn't have a Korean media, I wouldn't have a strong root to Korea. If I didn't watch Korean shows or dramas, I

wouldn't improve my Korean. [When I began to watch Korean TV] I was like "This is something I am interested in" and I wanted it to be part of my culture. I took initiative. I learned Korean.

Many Korean Canadians interviewed for this book were able to understand Korean and thus had an advantage for enjoying the shows without fully relying on translations. For them, Korean TV was considered as a convenient means to learn more about their (ancestral) homeland. 22-year-old second generation Jim commented, "Actually I would say the main reason I'm so good at speaking and understanding Korean is because of all the Korean media that I have been watching."

The diasporic youth's familiarity with Korean language and culture, as well as childhood exposure to Korean TV in the home, may not necessarily lead to their continued viewing of Korean TV. In fact, several interviewees who used to access Korean media became less interested in it as their social circumstances changed. For example, Jeremy used to access a wide range of Korean TV content and Korean Internet portal sites such as Naver. However, after he entered the workforce, where he did not collaborate with Korean colleagues, the frequency of his Korean TV viewing and overall time-spent significantly decreased. In comparison with Jeremy, most of the interviewees continued watching Korean TV and navigating different TV content between English and Korean language programs. Overall, Korean TV was appealing cultural content and watching Korean TV was a common cultural practice among the young Korean Canadian interviewees. Korean dramas and entertainment shows were popular materials for them to maintain and enhance their ethnic identification and feeling at home.

Uniquely Korean

Many interviewees appreciated the unique attributes of Korean TV content. In particular, they found Korean TV accessible and relevant. According to 19-year-old Jeremy, who immigrated at the age of 4 and lived in Toronto, Korean TV was "more dynamic" compared to Canadian TV.

I think Korean TV programs are more dynamic and there is more happening and more dramatic than Canadian programming. Whether dramas or shows, Canadian programs are more toned down, whereas in Korean ones there's a lot going on constantly.

According to several interviewees, when compared with Western TV, Korean TV is not only dynamic, but also relatable. They identified with Korean TV—its characters, stories, language, and culture. For example, 22-year-old second generation Jim in Vancouver preferred K-dramas to American dramas: "there's something different about Korean dramas than the American dramas." He supposed the creators might be "so good at portraying how the people are feeling and that makes the audience feel that it's very relatable. Even though I'm not born and raised in Korea." The feeling of relevance further reinforces the viewers' ethnic identification. Grace, a university student in Vancouver, liked Korean TV's ordinary and comfortable content and themes.

> I like Korean shows a bit more than Western shows, because they are more PG [Parental Guidance suggested; i.e., not explicitly adult-oriented materials]. So you can watch the shows with all sorts of people, like seniors or children. They don't swear on TV, right. So it's very interesting. And the celebrities seem like everyday people, so it's easier to relate to them, and it's nice to hear about how they interact with their family, interact with their friends, interact with fans.

Grace's account illustrates cultural proximity between diasporic youth and their homeland media. In fact, K-dramas have appealed to a range of audience members by their facilitation of "transnational affective intimacies," which is identified as an appealing factor (M. J. Lee 2019, p. 41).

For those regularly watching Korean TV, K-dramas and entertainment shows offered a sense of belonging and local affects that they may not frequently feel in their current homeland of Canada. Emma, who immigrated at the age of 2, appreciated her constant access to Korean TV, which she had enjoyed for a long time. She found Korean content more relevant and interesting than its Western counterpart. Emma distinguished Korean TV from Western shows in terms of feelings of intimate affection (*jeong*).

> Korean TV is more personal. Korean talk shows more about people's everyday life. They are a lot more open about it but Canadian or American

shows are more like outer topic, a little less of their personal life. Korean ones are more like about stories full of *jeong* [i.e., deep, intimate affection].

In comparison with Emma who left Korea at a very early age without any memory about the country, several 1.5 generation interviewees who had relatively concrete memories of their homeland of Korea engaged with Korean TV to fulfill their nostalgic desire and sense of ethnic identity. For example, 22-year-old Torontonian Kevin stated:

Watching Korean TV brings me memories about Korea. Definitely watching those shows help. It's funny. Even though I am more comfortable with Canadian culture, I still wanna be informed or exposed to Korean culture too. I am a dedicated watcher. It's my routine.

In this manner, for the 1.5 generation youth who were "not White-washed" (their own term), watching Korean TV was often incorporated into their daily home routines.

Interestingly, a few interviewees noted that they enjoyed watching Korean TV, but its plots (especially dramas) and storytelling techniques were somewhat "predictable" and "cheesy." Many interviewees pointed to cliché in Korean TV. A few interviewees seemed to lose their interest in K-drama due to the cliché, whereas many others still enjoyed the cliché. Slow-burn, soft-touch, romantic dramas were noted by the interviewees as a signature K-drama convention. Such conventions were described by some as clichés and as unique attributes by others. Regarding his favorite K-dramas, 19-year-old Noah described Korean romantic drama conventions as follows: "The romance scenes [in Korean TV] are a lot different [from Western TV shows]. They are really suspended in a way where, it's like, nothing really happens and if they happen to kiss it's such a big deal. It's K-drama style. As to Western shows, if it's just a kiss, it's just a kiss, right?" Overall, the interviewees who regularly or frequently watched Korean TV agreed that K-drama involves slow-burn, drawn-out romance and clichés, yet is interesting enough, especially compared to mainstream American TV. The use of clichés may reduce viewers' interest; however, as H. Lee's (2018) study suggested, K-drama fans tended to appreciate the clichés if the K-drama clichés are deployed strategically and creatively. Moreover, H. Lee (2018) also showed that the fans find predictability is "part of the charm" of K-drama. Similarly, for the diasporic young people in this book, K-drama cliché was considered as an interesting genre convention. The explicit clichés, however, seemed to distinguish K-drama from American counterparts and thus ironically contributed to the diasporic youth's appreciation of Korean TV's uniqueness.

Speaking about uniquely Korean aspects of Korean TV, several interviewees also pointed out some negative aspects in Hallyu media. That is, while certain values represented in Korean TV were highly regarded, such as respect for elders and family-oriented norms, other aspects were considered backward and unacceptable, such as an overemphasis on people's appearances and patriarchal norms. The aforementioned Grace, a fan of Hallyu media, was particularly critical of the lookism and misogynist discourses that she noticed in some Korean TV shows.

> I especially hate it when a lot of women are picked on for their looks. Some comedians always get picked on for their appearance. And then the comedians in such shows as *Gag Concert* [a Korean comedy show that aired between 1999 and 2020] and *Happy Together* [a Korean talk show that aired between 2001 and 2020] usually just have to laugh it off. I find that it's not acceptable that they do it. (…) I stopped watching *Happy Together* once the female cast [who was often picked on for her appearance] left. Because then I felt like it wasn't very fair for them anymore for the women in the Korean entertainment industry. So I stopped watching it.

For many female interviewees, the beauty standards shown in Korean TV and Korean media industries were highly problematic. 16-year-old Kimberly was critical: "I don't think I like the beauty standard that they have, such as the lighter skins. You have to have a certain body weight and a certain height, and train yourself to look like that." The heavy emphasis on unrealistic beauty standards, which do not reflect ordinary Koreans at all (e.g., the emphasis on extremely white skin), was criticized by most of the interviewees and by critics as well (Park and Hong 2021).

There are ongoing debates about the conventions of narrative Hallyu media and their ideological implications. Whereas Korean TV has been recognized for its innovative format and storytelling (Chung 2019), its cliché-filled conventions and conservative and escapist content include misogynic, patriarchal, and/or racist representation (An 2022). Equipped with linguistic and cultural literacy that allows for accessing English and Korean cultural texts, diasporic Korean youth decode Hallyu in relation to other cultural materials available to them, such as Anglophone TV dramas and mainstream Hollywood movies (D. C. Oh 2015). Thus, through these bicultural navigations and lens, they do not always and wholeheartedly celebrate transnational Korean media. For example, they are critical of certain aspects of Hallyu, such as Korean entertainment shows' misogynistic jokes and the K-pop industry's emphasis on idols' appearances. In this regard, Yoon (2020) has defined young Korean Canadians as a particularly *selective* and *critical* audience group of Hallyu, especially in comparison with older first generation immigrants who habitually and/or nostalgically consume Korean media.

Intimate and Cool

Korean TV offers a window through which diasporic youth can virtually immerse themselves in the distant (ancestral) homeland and make transnational connections with their ethnic roots. Through Korean TV, diasporic Korean youth fantasize about and engage with their ancestral home not only as a place of ethnic roots but also as a metropolitan, urban location of playful and cutting-edge popular culture. By engaging with Korean TV, the young people associated Korea with several images including highly urbanized (yet still intimate) city life, K-pop merchandise shops, intimate traditional markets, and food trucks that sell various street foods. In particular, K-dramas and entertainment shows sometimes offer the diasporic viewers the fantasy of a highly advanced pop cultural metropolis (Y. Oh 2018). Paige, a 21-year-old second generation in Vancouver, noted that K-dramas make her and her peers desire to go to Korea: "Korean TV is always promoting Korea. Even in dramas they have such a beautiful scenery. So they're always portraying a good image of Korea. Because when you see something on TV you want to go there. And I definitely get that from Korean media."

Especially for those unable to make trips to Korea, K-dramas and entertainment shows offer a window to contemporary Korean society. 21-year-old Rebecca was largely influenced by K-dramas to make a trip to Korea.

> The people you see on TV are just a small tiny percentage of the actual population. I went there. Not everyone looked like they were beautiful [like in K-dramas]. And they didn't dress like they were on the runway. Everyone was just kind of the same in semi-formal and you see girls wearing blouses and skirts. And really really simple. Everyone had the same

color hair. It was different because I thought that there would be so much more color and diversity.

What she saw on the screen was different from what she experienced and observed during her pilgrimage to Korea. Not unlike any other pop culture pilgrimage, until her recent trip to Seoul, she fantasized about Korea, to some extent. The diasporic youth's imagination of Korea is of course different from some non-Korean Hallyu fans' fetishization of the country as purely a fantasy land. As noted by Rebecca above, young Korean Canadians sooner or later realized what was behind this mediated Korea as an intimate *and* cool location, through experiences of physically being there or triangulating different sources (e.g., communication with Korean Canadian peers or family members).

Intimate imagination of a (physically distant, ancestral) homeland is often enabled through particular conventions and formats, wherein cool, youthful K-pop stars appear on Korean TV and tell their stories. It is common for K-pop idols to appear as guests in Korean entertainment shows or other genres (Jin 2019; J. O. Kim 2019).[6] K-pop idols' appearances in other genres attract K-pop fans to Korean TV to explore their favorite idols' personal aspects beyond their singing and dancing onstage. Korean entertainment—variety shows, called *yeneung*—plays a pivotal role in the transmedia storytelling of Hallyu, as they allow celebrities to intimately speak about themselves and their performance in other genres, such as K-pop and K-drama. Julia, a 21-year-old student in Toronto who immigrated at the age of 6, described the appeal of *yeneung*.

> Well, right now I watch *yeneung*. In Korean *yeneung*, you bring the celebrities on but here (in Canadian TV) it's not so much. It's regular people come on go jump around like mazes. I don't know what is Canadian counterpart to *yeneung*. It's just funny and it has people that I recognize - celebrities that I like in Korean TV. Korean ones are more involved with

---

[6] Hallyu industries have extensively deployed digital media platforms for global dissemination of content, especially in a more digitally-driven period of Hallyu, known as Hallyu 2.0 or New Korean Wave (Jin 2016). In particular, by deploying various digital media forms synergistically, the industries have maximized the effects of media convergence. One content is remediated in many different forms and a source is sold through multiple platforms. This advancement in remediation and convergence (Jenkins 2004; Madianou and Miller 2013) has also served to facilitate overseas fans' participation in, and interaction with, the universe of Hallyu—through uploading and sharing of user-generated content, translation, and commenting.

celebrities and more involved with showcasing them, whereas American and Canadian reality shows are more about just common people.

The entertainment show genre has been a unique component of Hallyu media. As Julia pointed out, its diversity and experimentation have been so stimulating that many shows' formats have been exported to Asian and Western countries. Idols often appear on the shows to promote their new songs; however, they participate in various activities rather than simply talking. They take part in sports/game competitions and/or present personal skills/talents (*gaeingi*). The appearance of K-pop idols across different Hallyu genres has been reinforced and driven by Hallyu entertainment companies' one-source, multiuse strategies (Seo 2012). For example, *Running Man*, an action game show set in urban landmarks in Korea, has been particularly popular among Asian youth partly due to the frequent appearance of popular idol guests and the completion of missions through collaboration and competition with the host and other guest members. As shown by K-pop idols' presence across different TV genres, Korean TV's transmedia storytelling facilitates diasporic young people's reception of Hallyu media across different genres, including K-pop, and reinforces their involvement in the universe of Hallyu media. Overall, the young Korean Canadians tended to easily identify with cultural components that characterize Korea—such as respect for elders and intimate sociality (*jeong*)—through Korean TV. For the diasporic youth, Korean TV was comprised of intimate and cool yet easily identifiable cultural components that allowed them to engage with Korea "there" from "here" in Canada.

Communal and Participatory Viewing

Diasporic viewing of Korean TV often involves communal and participatory viewing practices. According to the interviewees, K-dramas and entertainment shows were often viewed in a communal setting, in which diasporic sociality is reinforced. The communal viewing means not only physical togetherness but also virtual (or emotional) togetherness through the sharing of individual viewer responses to a show with others (often through online communications).

Nicole, a 26-year-old nurse, recalled her childhood in Vancouver: "Back then the Internet wasn't really developed. So my mom would rent

Korean drama DVDs and we would watch it. So she did enjoy them a lot. My mom and I would sit together and watch the whole series. I remember that it was fun times." Such communal, family viewing experiences appeared to continue in the later high-speed, wireless Internet period through streaming sites (and sometimes projected on TV sets in the living room). 16-year-old Samuel, who is a dedicated viewer of K-drama, described his viewing patterns.

> My mom loves K-drama. And when she's watching it, I like to watch it with her because she would have it playing when she's sitting down and just come over. And when it looks fun, I just watch it. She tells me what the title of the drama so I can watch it later. There's also a great selection of K-drama on Netflix. So I just like when I'm bored, I just click on random drama and just start watching it. My mom watched *The Descendants of the Sun* when it was popular. She watched it first and she fell in love with the actor. After she watched it, I decided to watch it. And it was really fun. And we both watched it and then we discussed it, like how this came so popular and how, and what the next story is going to be.

In this manner, viewing together was a popular practice among Korean Canadian youth in this book. They were commonly introduced to Korean TV dramas in family or peer group contexts. Compared to K-pop, which the young people were introduced to via social media, K-drama was relatively a family-oriented genre that family members often viewed together. Moreover, for many interviewees, Korean TV was an important topic for small talk between Korean Canadian youth in school. 22-year-old Jim recalled his school days when he enjoyed speaking about Korean entertainment shows from the previous night, often exclusively with other Korean Canadian peers.

> I would say Korean TV gives you something to talk about. Because you couldn't go up to a White guy and say "Oh did you watch Kang Ho Dong [a Korean TV celebrity] screw up this week?" No you can't do that. They would be like "Who the hell is he?" (laughs) but fellow Korean Canadians all had been exposed to Korean TV. So it's something to talk about and to relate to.

For a few interviewees, K-drama's content itself was not necessarily far more interesting than that of American programs they also watched. However, they still kept watching Korean TV along with their family members or Korean Canadian friends because small talk about Korean TV constituted a component that facilitated their diasporic social networks. However, as they grew older, some interviewees no longer regularly watched Korean TV as their pattern of socializing changed. Rosie, for example, used to watch Korean TV with her sister and/or parents but was no longer very interested in K-dramas because she found American shows far more interesting. She recalled that Korean TV viewing was a family practice: "When I watched Korean TV a lot, it had a lot to do with my family (whose members often watched Korean TV)." She also added that her Korean friends in her school in Vancouver were also an influential factor: "And it was also affected by the types of friends. Because you would gradually come to school and then talk about what you watched and then you'd make small talks and then you would gradually just connect more with Korean people." According to Rosie, who was a university student at the time of the interview, her media consumption became more individualized when speaking about particular TV content was no longer crucial for socializing.

> Now most of my friends are people I've known for a while and so we don't need to really talk about that [particular TV content]. Even if we watch completely different things we can still be friends (laughs). But I feel like initially it will affect what people spend time with.

Rosie's accounts confirm that K-drama (and probably K-pop) would enable or restrict Korean Canadians' participation in particular peer networks.

In addition to communal viewing, another practice of diasporic viewing of Korean TV involves participatory viewing. That is, a few young people interviewed for this book, who were relatively dedicated to Hallyu media and willing to promote the content widely, provided their labor to create paratexts about Korean TV. Despite being small in number among the entire sample of interview participants, these young people translated Korean texts to English, made comments on fan forums or social media platforms, and generated reaction videos or accessed others' reaction videos. Indeed, since the rise of Hallyu in North America, bilingual 1.5 generation Korean Canadians (and Korean Americans) are known for their contribution to fansubbing communities (Dwyer 2017; Hu 2010). While most of the young people interviewed for this book were dedicated audiences of Hallyu media, a limited number of interviewees actively contributed to paratext production, such as fansubbing or vlogging. Grace was one of the most active fan audience members among the interviewees. As an undergraduate student interested in writing and literature, she often contributed to translating Korean media content into English. As an enthusiast of Hallyu media, she considered herself a promoter of Hallyu to international audiences.

> Every week or every day I would try to translate something and work on it for an hour and submit. And for *Produce 101* [K-pop audition program that aired every Friday night in Korea in 2016], because it was a weekly show. Every Saturday [in the Canadian time zone], the show came up. And then Sundays and Mondays, I would try to finish everything. Not the whole show but 10 minutes of it, 20 minutes of it and then write that script and then whoever is in charge of putting the subtitles on, they do their task. And then we try to get it out of the week.

Participatory consumption such as fansubbing is a way in which Korean Canadians apply their "second generation advantages" (Kasinitz et al. 2008) as bilingual speakers and translators. In the emerging youth culture of Hallyu, their bicultural literacy, which otherwise would remain invisible, can potentially obtain cultural currency and thus be registered as a form of cultural capital. Global fan audiences of Hallyu have been known for their enthusiastic production of paratexts and various reactions to the original texts (e.g., reaction videos) (Jin et al. 2021). Among the audience groups, diasporic Koreans equipped with bilingual and bicultural knowledge are in a unique position as cultural translators who can mediate "there" and "here." Indeed, as addressed earlier in this chapter, some streaming platforms (Viki in particular) have benefited from diasporic Koreans' contributions to their rapid growth.

Overall, the young Korean Canadians tended to be exposed to Korean TV through communal and participatory viewing experiences, and kept watching so that they could have small talk with others. Transnational Korean media contributes to constructing diasporic sociality. It is true that Korean media has been available in Canada through legal or illegal routes for decades, and thus, the interviewees' parents frequently accessed Korean TV. However, the recent rise of Hallyu and its extensive exploitation of digital technology substantially changed the what and how of diasporic media—the quality and quantity of Korean media available in Canada (and globally) are now unprecedented with the emergence of digitally-driven Hallyu (also referred to as Hallyu 2.0) since the 2010s (Jin 2016). Digital Hallyu allowed diasporic youth to omnivorously navigate different media content, across different genres, regardless of its nationality. They can opt in and opt out of the universe of Hallyu, without being exclusively committed or immersed in Korean TV. In this period of digitally-driven Hallyu, diasporic youth may explore ethnic and cultural options in their cultural consumption. In so doing, they may articulate their diasporic lens through which both return to ethnic culture and compliance with the White-dominant cultural frame may be challenged and juggled. Through Korean TV, the diasporic youth "feel at home" and explore new senses of "home," as they encounter new modes of representation beyond the White-dominant Western mediascape.

New Territories of Korean TV

Diasporic young Koreans affirm their ethnic connections through their transnational consumption of Korean narrative media, including dramas, entertainment shows, and films, all of which are made in Korea and are increasingly available online. While these media forms are comprehensively referred to as "Korean TV" in this chapter, the Korean narrative media enjoyed by the diasporic youth was not limited to made-in-Korea content. There are other forms of narrative media that can still be categorized as Korean TV. The Korean narrative media genres of Hallyu have been hybridized in several different forms. For example, North American remakes of original Korean entertainment shows, such as *King of Mask Singer*, can be considered part of Hallyu-influenced media (Jin et al. 2021). In this regard, this section examines two examples of new forms of Korean TV: (a) Western media texts incorporating explicitly Korean themes and/or developed by (diasporic) Korean talents and (b) lifestyle vlogs by ordinary Koreans, which are not produced by conventional media industries. These new genre forms of narrative media appear to increasingly appeal to diasporic youth as they explore ethnic identification and new modes of representation through their bicultural lens and navigations of these new genres. Moreover, these genres contribute to expanding the scope of Hallyu, which may no longer be defined simply by its physical location of origin but rather involves diverse routes and multi-layered textuality.

TV of Diasporic Koreans: Kim's Convenience

The young Korean Canadians interviewed for this book frequently accessed Korean TV, although they do not necessarily remain dedicated to it. Interestingly, compared to transnational media from Korea, the young people's interest in locally produced ethnic Korean media, such as Korean language newspapers or TV programs produced locally, was almost absent. The absence of ethnic media in diasporic youth's media consumption may be due to the weak infrastructure of ethnic Korean TV production in Canada.[7] Locally-grown ethnic media without solid revenue structures tend to rely on local sponsors and are under the pressure of commodification (Jin and Kim 2011). In particular, Korean ethnic media produced in Canada have extremely limited resources for producing its content (Jin and Kim 2011; Yu 2018). Given the lack of original and locally relevant content in ethnic media run by Korean Canadian communities, Canadian network TV's introduction of Korean themes in its programming may provide an option for diasporic Korean audiences to engage with their stories on their screens. In this regard, the recent production and popularity of the mainstream Canadian TV show, *Kim's Convenience* (2016–2021), which may not be explicitly categorized as Korean TV or Hallyu media, reveals how the stories and storytelling of Korean diasporas are incorporated into their "host" countries' popular media and public imagination.

As briefly mentioned in earlier chapters, media representation of Koreans or East Asians has been extremely rare in the Canadian mediascape. It was only in the mid-2010s when Canadian network TV aired its first East Asian-led sitcom, *Kim's Convenience*. A few interviewees pointed out the CBC's hit comedy *Kim's Convenience* as a rare (if not the only) example of the portrayal of Korean communities and their culture in Canada. *Kim's Convenience* is a popular Canadian sitcom about a Korean Canadian family running a convenience store in Toronto. Based on the stage play by Korean Canadian playwright Ins Choi, who participated in its TV version as a co-creator, this TV sitcom has been reviewed positively by Canadian audiences and released in many other countries including Korea. The show has been so acclaimed by Canadian critics

---

[7] Although there are Korean language newspapers in Canada, they have limited resources and readership. Thus, the ethnic newspapers do not necessarily play a significant journalistic role (Jin and Kim 2011).

that it won several TV awards, including main star Paul Sun-Hyung Lee's 2017 and 2018 wins at the Canadian Screen Awards for Best Lead Actor in a Comedy. Lee's 2018 award acceptance speech has attracted media attention and went viral. In the speech, he noted, "Representation matters because when communities and people see themselves reflected up on the screens, it is an inspiring and very powerful moment for them." The show has been acclaimed for its representation of Korean and Asian Canadian communities as emphasized in Lee's speech.

Interestingly, while *Kim's Convenience*, not unlike many other Canadian shows, was not particularly popular among those interviewed, some interviewees watched more than several episodes of the show and there were mixed responses. Some viewers evaluated this show favorably as a long-awaited, welcome addition with which they can identify as it portrays Korean Canadians who are almost absent in Canadian media. For example, 22-year-old Meghan enjoyed the show as she was pleasantly surprised by the portrayal of Korean Canadians: "Growing up, I didn't think there was any Korean portrayal in Canadian TV. It was really weird for me when Korean things did start to pop up in Western media, like 'Gangnam Style.' But now it feels more normal to me. *Kim's Convenience* was popular and I loved it." More specifically, 16-year-old Sherry who watched the entire first season of the show appreciated the way in which the show humorously and vividly portrayed Korean immigrants in Canada.

> (Interviewer: Do you watch Canadian TV programs?) I think I have only watched one Canadian TV show, *Kim's Convenience* by CBC. Everything else is always staged in America. (Interviewer: How was *Kim's Convenience*?) I definitely liked the show because they kind of reminded me a lot of my family (laughs) and it was like the whole plot of an immigrant family from Korea in Canada. So, yeah, I was really enjoying to watch it.

In comparison, a few other viewers had mixed feelings about the show because they thought the show's Korean characters were stereotypical. 24-year-old Stella, who was born and grew up with Korean immigrant parents running a small business, critically noted:

> Yes, it's cool that they're trying to make the immigration life into TV, but at the same time as I was watching it, I thought they were highlighting all the Asian stereotypes... so, I didn't really like. They were trying to be

funny (…) but, for us it's not really funny, because I know the hardships and all the stuff behind immigrant families.

Given the overall positive reviews for the show in mainstream Canadian media, Stella's response was somewhat unique. She seemed to receive this show emotionally because it reminded her of her family's struggles with settling in Canada. As Stella pointed out, the characters in *Kim's Convenience* are comically portrayed and can be seen as stereotypical.

There have been questions about the representation of Korean and Asian immigrants on *Kim's Convenience*. In response to criticism that the show may reproduce a stereotypical portrayal of Korean Canadian families to some extent, the showrunner and cast, along with many viewers and critics, argued that the show's Asian representation does not draw on stereotypes but rather on archetypes that are often adopted for the effective delivery of stories and characters in the 20-min-per-episode sitcom format. Indeed, reportedly, the show is based on Ins Choi's experiences as a second generation Korean who grew up in an immigrant family in Toronto (Westerman 2019).[8]

Moreover, a few interviewees considered the show to be neither a Korean nor a Western sitcom. They distinguished the show from Korean TV (made in Korea) and Hallyu media. For 16-year-old 1.5 generation Samuel, *Kim's Convenience* was an "American style show" about Korean immigrants.

---

[8] The co-creator Ins Choi and the main star Paul Sun-Hyung Lee noted that the characterization involves archetypes rather than stereotypes. However, as the show progressed, stereotypical and limited representation of Korean characters was also pointed out by the cast. In particular, Jean Yoon, who played the mother of the family, and Simu Liu, who played the son Jung, both admitted respectively that the portrayal of Korean and Asian characters in the show could be stereotypical. This limitation of the show seemed to be caused by the ways in which the show was written and produced. The production team was predominantly White, although the show itself was based on Korean Canadian writer Ins Choi's original play and he was invited to be a co-creator and writer. According to Jean Yoon, Ins Choi seemed to have limited control of the show's running, and the production team did not communicate with the Korean cast. In response to the showrunner's abrupt announcement of the discontinuation of the show after five exceptionally successful seasons, Yoon noted, "The big lesson for me is that you cannot do a show about a minority experience, have it run by a white person and expect it to be OK. Sometimes the white mainstream think when we ask for equity, we just want the jobs. But this affects the intrinsic moral values of the work we do. A lack of respect for a culture manifests as systemic racism" (C. Wang 2021).

> I feel like it was more American style than Korean style. And that, like, the dialog and storyline was kind of more similar to other American shows that I've watched. So I'm like, I don't really want to watch it because it's more American stuff. I kind of want to watch more Korean style.

Although Samuel did not elaborate, for him the show seemed more "American" (or Western) than Korean. That is, unlike Hallyu media content, this show about Korean Canadian lives did not sufficiently address contemporary Korean culture and popular culture. However, the show was considered not fully Western as well. The show did not follow trendy, fast-paced sitcom styles, with which young Canadian viewers might be familiar. As Hsu (2019, para 2) noted, the show offers a feeling of "watching an alternate time line" as "there is nothing edgy about the show." For this reason, *Kim's Convenience* may not be fully appealing to the young Korean Canadians in this book, and several initially enthusiastic viewers of the show discontinued watching. They enjoyed earlier seasons that portrayed Korean Canadians and tried to share diasporic stories. However, they felt the stories were no longer refreshing as the show continued throughout several seasons. 18-year-old Mia enjoyed the first two seasons of the show, but no longer watched the show.

> It was really popular when it came out and I think it's still popular. I'm not sure, though, because I stopped watching it, but I had a very positive response. I would watch it with my family occasionally. And I think kids at my school also enjoyed it a lot, too. Overall, there were positive reactions from the community. (Interviewer: Can I ask you what made you stop watching the show?) It's because I just found other shows that I was more interested in. Also, I think there was a small period of time where they stopped airing the show for a little bit to make more of a show. I began to watch other shows that were kind of more my style.[9]

As noted by Mia, some interviewees switched to other (primarily American or Korean) shows, which were "kind of more my style," as their interest in *Kim's Convenience* decreased. The show also did not seem to experiment with cutting-edge styles and themes, at least for some of the diasporic youth.

---

[9] While Season 1 and Season 2 aired in the fall seasons of 2016 and 2017, the later seasons aired at the beginning of January in 2019, 2020, and 2021. Thus, there was a longer break between Season 2 and Season 3.

Overall, as a rare mainstream TV program portraying a Korean immigrant family, *Kim's Convenience* has been largely welcomed and acclaimed by both critics and audiences. As shown in its fan forum on Reddit, the fans of the show (who named themselves "Kimbits") were enthusiastic about the show's vivid diasporic storytelling and urged the reconsideration of its abrupt cancelation in 2021. However, as the Asian Canadian main cast members' interviews reveal, the production of the show had recurring problems with representing cultural diversity (C. Wang 2021). It is important that despite its half-success as the first Canadian sitcom portraying Korean diaspora it opened a door for further development of diasporic media. Hopefully, young Korean Canadian talents and audiences will engage with mainstream media industries to develop and popularize new shows about diasporic Korean experiences.

Personal Broadcasting or Vlogging

With the flood of user-generated content on digital platforms and social media, ordinary people's daily video diaries (referred to as vlogs) have integrated into the cultural flows of Hallyu. Although Hallyu has been primarily known by its content designed and made by major entertainment corporations, an increasing number of ordinary digital users have contributed to expanding the cultural repertoire of Hallyu. In comparison with the dominant, industry-led cultural wave, this new territory of Hallyu is led by ordinary people who, without now being able to engage with digital technology, would have remained somewhat invisible in the receiving end of transnational cultural flows. Some end-users have redefined themselves as creators by taking part in the emerging digital wave of Hallyu and in so doing are adding a new layer of user-driven Hallyu that moves beyond the cultural circulation of industry-designed, ready-made products (Jin et al. 2021). The rapid increase in personal broadcasting or vlogging activities via YouTube and other streaming platforms has been a recent development in digitally-driven participatory culture—especially among Hallyu audiences. In particular, vlogging practices have become exponentially widespread in Korea's mediascape and are now an integral part of the digital phase of Hallyu.

The young Korean Canadians in this book viewed Korean vlogs for several reasons. Most of all, they were curious about the daily lives of contemporary Koreans. 16-year-old Samuel, who left Korea at the age of

6, followed several Korean YouTubers to get a sense of what was going on in Korea.

> I follow some Korean vloggers on YouTube. I like watching them. I wanted to watch the Korean vlogs because I was kind of really curious on what Korea looks like right now. So I watch those YouTube [channels] and their contents were actually sometimes really good and were kind of interesting. So I kind of got the experience of how Koreans live right now in this day and age. So I can kind of get a better understanding.

For those who identify with their ethnic roots and desire to maintain their transnational connection with Korea, it seems important to keep up with ordinary people's stories. In comparison, Emily, a 25-year-old second generation, wanted to explore cultural differences between the two cultures by watching Korean YouTubers' challenges in experiencing North American culture.

> There are a few YouTube channels where Koreans try out North America things or talk about their thoughts about other countries. I thought that was kind of an interesting series. I think it would give North Americans a better idea of what Korean people more like.

In this manner, in addition to mainstream Hallyu media, such as K-pop, K-drama, and Korean entertainment shows, the digital storytelling of ordinary people through vlogging appeared to be a popular genre for the diasporic youth to engage with their ethnic roots on the one hand and to address their cultural tastes that are not fulfilled by mainstream Western TV or Korean TV on the other.

According to the interviewees, Korean vlogs were appealing primarily because of their unique content, which was distinguished from that of Canadian or American vlogs. Several young women interviewees, who followed Korean lifestyle vloggers, found that the Korean YouTubers offer more relevant tips for fashion, makeup, and home design. For example, given their skin tones and physical attributes, these young people preferred Korean vlogs to White creators' vlogs. The interviewees considered the YouTubers as "regular people" and thus easily identified with them. Vlogs appeared to offer the young people a window into a more intimate and ordinary life of their distant ethnic homeland. Moreover, vlogs are available more casually and easily accessible without any subscription or contextual knowledge.

Among various types of vlogs, live streaming eating shows, known as *meokbang* in Korea, were commonly viewed content and a popular pastime for some interviewees. *Meokbang*, a Korean portmanteau of "eating" and "broadcasting," has been particularly popular among young audiences in Korea's media environments. This genre has emerged as an exceptionally popular type of live streaming content among young people in Korea and increasingly in other countries. Many young broadcasters on YouTube, Twitch, or AfreecaTV (Korean streaming platform) have become micro-celebrities by exhibiting how they eat—often in extreme ways (e.g., eating an extremely large amount of food or extremely spicy foods).[10] 24-year-old Lucas frequently viewed a wide range of YouTube clips, many of which are Korean vlogs—from Army training reality shows to *meokbang*. When asked why he watched *meokbang* and why this genre may be popular, he commented, "They eat so much, so it's like impossible, it seems impossible, but they do it. So just being mesmerized by beating the unbeatable, OK?" For Lucas, watching Korean *meokbang* seemed to satisfy his interest in ordinary Koreans' daily lives and enabled him to visually enjoy the Korean foods he wanted to eat. As Hong and Park (2016) claimed, *meokbang* is popular in highly individualized Korea as it offers a feeling of filling up young generations' emotional hunger and provides the viewer with a vicarious pleasure of eating a lot without any concern about dietary disciplines and norms.

Some young people interviewed for this book accessed vlogs through different digital platforms without being limited to YouTube. 19-year-old Cody, who is a 1.5 generation in the workforce, often watched livestream broadcasting through AfreecaTV—the Korean platform that specializes in live streaming and personal broadcasting of gaming and *meokbang*. As a popular vlog genre in Korea, *meokbang* has been particularly popular on Korea-based streaming platforms like AfreecaTV. While YouTube was the most preferred platform for viewing vlogs, AfreecaTV was also used for those who are familiar with Korean language and Korean culture. The increasing number of overseas users of AfreecaTV may signal that Hallyu is not simply the flows of texts and content, but also involves

---

[10] Several *meokbang* YouTubers, who earn more than USD100,000 per month, have become micro-celebrities and role models for the post-millennial generation in Korea. While the popularity of food-related livestreams, such as social livestreams on Twitch, has been globally observed, *meokbang* is a unique cultural phenomenon that extensively incorporates mundane practices of eating into digital youth culture.

distribution of Korean media platforms to overseas users. In the transcultural flows of platforms, diasporic youth who are relatively familiar with the language and culture with which the Korean platforms operate may easily navigate by using their "second generation advantages" (Kasinitz et al. 2008) between different platforms (e.g., between YouTube and AfreecaTV). Given that "the shaping of digital stories is subject to mediation" (Lundby 2008, p. 12), the platform that is used and the elements of storytelling that are emphasized in a particular platform may influence how Korean personal broadcasting is transnationally consumed by diasporic youth. For example, an increasing number of YouTubers—especially those who are referred to as "influencers"—seem to make an effort to strategically create catchy content while branding their life as a commodity form (Khamis et al. 2017). In so doing, they seek to redefine themselves as micro-celebrities who are admired by their digital followers. For more systematic management, some YouTubers are affiliated with cultural intermediaries such as entertainment agencies or promoters to increase their audience bases and increase their power as influencers (Duffy 2017).

Viewing small screens that are streaming various "ordinary" people's lives, the diasporic youth may indirectly experience the highly competitive, fast-paced rhythms of the everyday lives of Seoulites. However, their motivation for engaging with the digital nirvana of personal broadcasting in the surge of Hallyu may be different from that of young Koreans. Cultural critics have argued that flourishing personal broadcasting practices in Korea has generated a unique youth culture drawn from the highly individualized lifestyles of the post-millennial generation, who cynically call themselves "*ingyeo*" or "human surplus/waste" (Hong and Park 2016; Song 2018). The culture of personal broadcasting also involves real-time interaction between vloggers and their viewers; AfreecaTV is a platform that exploits viewers' direct donation and contribution of digital currency (known as "*byeolpungsun*" that literally means star balloons) to their favorite vloggers (Choi 2019; Song 2018). That is, the personal broadcasting facilitates interactive and participatory communications, while reflecting the emotional landscape of a frustrated young generation under neoliberal competition.

It is unclear how much of the diasporic youth's engagement with Korean vlogs resonates with the precarious social atmosphere of highly neoliberalized Korea. However, diasporic young people's transnational viewing of vlogs reveals how national and transnational viewers are making diasporic connections and seeking answers to their own challenges in their transition to adulthood. For Korean Canadians, the viewing of and interacting with Korea-based, young vloggers may contribute to their cultural practices such as ethnic identification, looking for a refuge from the White-dominant cultural frame, and seeking new representations not referring to the White gaze.

CONCLUSION

Growing up as people of color in "multicultural" Canada, the Korean Canadians interviewed for this book rarely encountered media representation of diasporic Asians and their cultures. The Canadian mediascape has insufficiently engaged with non-White groups by firmly drawing on the White-dominant cultural frame. For the diasporic Korean Canadian youth, Hallyu media appeared to offer them more relevant cultural resources, with which they could navigate different cultural content and modes of storytelling and engage with the question of identity in between different cultures. Through their viewing practices of Korean TV, diasporic youth engage with "there" (Korea) from "here" (Canada). In doing so, they further explore who they are and what is missing in the White-dominant Canadian mediascape.

For most of the young Korean Canadians in this book, Korean TV was considered to be more relevant compared to American and Canadian TV. Although they were more familiar with English than Korean and were accustomed to Canadian social contexts, they sought ethno-racial identification through the Hallyu media and looked for what they felt was missing in Canadian and Western media—values such as intimate feelings of *jeong* or respect for elders. In so doing, the young people appeared to negotiate their uncertain feelings about their national identity and sense of belonging and to explore a bicultural lens through which different modes of storytelling co-exist and are even hybridized as cultural resources for their lives in between two cultures.

The diasporic viewing of Korean TV by the interviewees reveals the ways in which Hallyu is integrated into young Korean Canadians' everyday contexts. In the midst of White-dominant media representation, the increasing global availability and popularity of Korean TV may provide the diasporic youth with meaningful momentum for exploring who they are and how they can critically navigate between different cultural texts and contexts. It should be noted that although Hallyu media has been described as relevant, relatable, participatory, and cutting-edge, it is not inherently progressive or counter-hegemonic. As the interviewees some-times pointed out, Korean TV reveals its regressive ideological positions (e.g., misogynic themes in some Korean entertainment or comedy shows). Some women interviewees were particularly critical of the lack of gender sensitivity in Korean TV. Moreover, while the diasporic youth can identify with the stories and characters of Korean TV, the diasporic consumption of Hallyu media does not always enhance cultural space for the diasporic young people's stories and experiences. Of course, Hallyu media exploits digital media platforms that allow for extensive audience participation as evidenced in the interface of the Viki streaming site and vlogging on AfreecaTV. For example, watching a K-drama episode on Viki, a Korean Canadian viewer may share their thoughts with other anonymous viewers; a Korean Canadian viewer may send messages to *meokbang* influencers on AfreecaTV or YouTube to share their feelings. However, these partic-ipatory methods of consumption may not guarantee self-representation through which they tell about who they are.

Then, how can Korean Canadians tell and share their stories without consciously *explaining* who they are to others and the White-dominant society? As illustrated in Steven Yeun's interview at the beginning of the chapter, it is important for diasporic youth to exercise telling about who they are without self-monitoring and feelings of marginalization. Echoing Yeun's statement, the young people interviewed for this book appeared to explore opportunities and resources for their identity work through engaging with Hallyu media. By viewing Korean TV, Korean Canadians may become gradually aware that they do not have to explain who they are any more. Furthermore, through viewing Korean TV (and navigating between different narrative media from Korea, Canada, and elsewhere), the diasporic youth may feel at home where they are. Compared to the first generation who consume far more Korean media than Canadian media, diasporic young Koreans who are equipped with bilingual and bicultural literacy may actively navigate different media forms across "here" and "there." Moreover, diasporic media productions that contribute to representations of Korean identities may expand the scope of the Korean Wave. Canadian media's endeavor to introduce dias-poric Korean stories in *Kim's Convenience* is an important attempt, as it provided the diasporic viewers with the possibility of their stories being projected on the national mediascape. However, the show's abrupt cance-lation revealed that such experiments of diasporic storytelling are not an easy task given the existing dominant media structure.

Narrative media genres in Hallyu, such as K-drama, entertainment shows, films, and vlogs, have played a pivotal role in intra-Asian and global circulation of content from the once-peripheral Korean cultural industry. While K-pop has gained significant media attention owing to the megahits of a few K-pop idol groups, Hallyu is not limited to a genre but rather involves a wide range of storytelling (Jin et al. 2021). Certainly, digital media contributes to marginalized populations' self-representation and storytelling (Lundby 2008). However, only a limited number of young people interviewed for this book actually tried to do their own digital storytelling via YouTube and other platforms.[11] It is important to explore Korean Canadian voices in the Canadian mediascape and to examine further how diasporic individuals obtain and maintain the power to tell their stories through digital media and how such self-representation and storytelling can contribute to enhancing Korean Canadians' public engagement.

References

Aksoy, Asu, and Kevin Robins. 2000. Thinking across spaces: Transnational television from Turkey. *European Journal of Cultural Studies* 3 (3): 343–365.

An, Ji-yoon. 2022. Aliens, mermaids and cartoons: Neoliberal gender politics in twenty-first-century South Korean dramas. In *Imagining "we" in the age of "I": Romance and social bonding in contemporary culture*, ed. Mary Harrod, Suzanne Leonard, and Diane Negra, 110–126. London: Routledge.

[11] Although not addressed in this chapter, vlogs created by Korean Canadians themselves constitute a narrative media genre that can be considered for further studies of diasporic Korean youth experiences and representation. Among the interview participants, only a few had created and uploaded their own videos (e.g., dance cover videos and fansubtitles) on publicly available platforms. Rather than creating their own content, interviewees tended to view other diasporic Korean or Asian vlogs. According to the interview participants, compared to the rapidly increasing number of popular Korean American YouTubers, the number and viewership of Korean Canadian vloggers are relatively marginal. A few Korean Canadians have been recognized on social media as "influencers." For example, Daniel Kim, a Vancouver-based Korean Canadian YouTuber in his thirties, has been an influential figure for over a decade. His pop music edit/remix videos, a series titled Pop Danthology, went viral in the early 2010s. As a university graduate and K-pop star wannabe, he went to Korea to explore his career options and even participated in a K-pop audition program, which turned out to be unsuccessful (Korea Herald 2014; Soh 2017). After career and emotional struggles, global media attention to his Pop Danthology made him an influencer and motivational speaker.

Brah, Avtar. 1996. *Cartographies of diaspora: Contesting identities*. London: Routledge.

Canadian Press. 2012. Asian-looking woman scientist image rejected for $100 bills. *CBC News*, August 17. https://www.cbc.ca/news/politics/asian-loo king-woman-scientist-image-rejected-for-100-bills-1.1183360.

Choi, Ji-won. 2019. Massive donation to female streamer stirs up internet in Korea. *The Korea Herald*, July 31. http://www.koreaherald.com/view.php?ud=20190731000742.

Choi, JungBong, and Roald Maliangkay, eds. 2015. *K-Pop: The international rise of the Korean music industry*. London: Routledge.

Chua, Beng Huat, and Koichi Iwabuchi, eds. 2008. *East Asian pop culture: Analysing the Korean Wave*. Hong Kong: Hong Kong University Press.

Chung, Elaine. 2019. Chinese-Korean TV drama co-production: Representations of international romance and the potential of multiculturalism. In *The rise of K-dramas: Essays on Korean television and its global consumption*, ed. Jae Yoon Park and Ann-Gee Lee, 154–172. Jefferson: McFarland & Company, Inc.

Cruz, Angela Gracia B., Yuri Seo, and Itir Binay. 2021. Cultural globalization from the periphery: Translation practices of English-speaking K-pop fans. *Journal of Consumer Culture* 21 (3): 638–659.

Duffy, Brooke Erin. 2017. *(Not) getting paid to do what you love: Gender, social media, and aspirational work*. New Haven: Yale University Press.

Dwyer, Tessa. 2017. *Speaking in subtitles: Revaluing screen translation*. Edinburgh: Edinburgh University Press.

Dyer, Richard. 1997. *White*. London: Routledge.

Fleras, Augie. 2011. *The media gaze: Representations of diversities in Canada*. Vancouver: UBC Press.

Frater, Patrick. 2021. China poised to give Korean content a boost after three year boycott. *Variety*, March 3. https://variety.com/2021/film/asia/china-giving-korean-content-boost-after-boycott-1234920540.

Fuhr, Michael. 2016. *Globalization and popular music in South Korea: Sounding out K-pop*. London: Routledge.

Gillespie, Marie. 1995. *Television, ethnicity and cultural change*. London: Routledge.

Han, Benjamin M. 2019. Fantasies of modernity: Korean TV dramas in Latin America. *Journal of Popular Film and Television* 47 (1): 39–47.

Henthorn, Jamie. 2019. International fan professionalization on Viki. *Television & New Media* 20 (5): 525–538.

Hong, Seok-Kyeong. 2020. *BTS on the road*. Seoul: Across [in Korean].

Hong, Seok-Kyeong, and Sojeong Park. 2016. Emergence of internet *mukbang* (foodcasting) and its hegemonic process in media culture. *Media & Society* 24 (1): 105–150 [in Korean].

Hsu, Hua. 2019. "Kim's convenience," the genial Canadian sitcom that feels like watching another time line. *The New Yorker*, August 28. https://www.newyorker.com/recommends/watch/kims-convenience-the-genial-canadian-sitcom-that-feels-like-watching-another-time-line.

Hu, Brian. 2010. Korean TV serials in the English-language diaspora: Translating difference online and making it racial. *The Velvet Light Trap* 66: 36–49.

Jenkins, Henry. 2004. The cultural logic of media convergence. *International Journal of Cultural Studies* 7 (1): 33–43.

Jin, Dal Yong. 2016. *New Korean Wave: Transnational cultural power in the age of social media*. Champaign: University of Illinois Press.

Jin, Dal Yong. 2019. Transmedia storytelling in the age of digital media: East Asian perspectives. *International Journal of Communication* 13: 2085–2093.

Jin, Dal Yong, and Soochul Kim. 2011. Sociocultural analysis of the commodification of ethnic media and Asian consumers in Canada. *International Journal of Communication* 5: 552–569.

Jin, Dal Yong, Kyong Yoon, and Wonjung Min. 2021. *Transnational Hallyu: The globalization of Korean digital and popular culture*. Lanham: Rowman & Littlefield.

Ju, Hyejung. 2020. Korean TV drama viewership on Netflix: Transcultural affection, romance, and identities. *Journal of International and Intercultural Communication* 13 (1): 32–48.

Ju, Hyejung. 2021. K-dramas meet Netflix: New models of collaboration with the digital West. In *The soft power of the Korean Wave: Parasite, BTS and drama*, ed. Youna Kim, 171–183. London: Routledge.

Jun, Hannah. 2017. Hallyu at a crossroads: The clash of Korea's soft power success and China's hard power threat in light of Terminal High Altitude Area Defence (THAAD) System deployment. *Asian International Studies Review* 18 (1): 153–169.

Kasinitz, Philip, John H. Mollenkopf, Mary C. Waters, and Jennifer Holdaway. 2008. *Inheriting the city: The children of immigrants come of age*. New York: Russell Sage Foundation.

Khamis, Susie, Lawrence Ang, and Raymond Welling. 2017. Self-branding 'micro-celebrity' and the rise of Social Media Influencers. *Celebrity Studies* 8 (2): 191–208.

Kim, Christine. 2016. *The minor intimacies of race: Asian publics in North America*. Champaign: University of Illinois Press.

Kim, Minyoung. 2021. Riding the K-wave, Netflix spotlights stories made in Korea and watched by the world. https://about.netflix.com/en/news/riding-the-k-wave-netflix-spotlights-stories-made-in-korea-and-watched-by.

Kim, Ju Oak. 2019. The storyteller who crosses boundaries in Korean reality television: Transmedia storytelling in new journey to the west. *International Journal of Communication* 13: 2143–2160.

Kim, Tae-Sik. 2020. Young migrant Vietnamese in the Czech Republic reflect diasporic contexts in their identification of cultural proximity with Korean media. *Journal of Intercultural Studies* 41 (4): 524–539.

Kim, Kyung Hyun, and Tian Li. 2018. Running Man: The Korean television variety program on the transnational, affective run. *Telos* 184: 163–184.

Korea Foundation for International Cultural Exchange. 2021. *The annual survey of overseas Hallyu*. Seoul: Korea Foundation for International Cultural Exchange (KOFICE) [in Korean].

Korea Herald. 2014. Herald interview: The mind behind 'pop danthology'. *The Korea Herald*, December 29. http://www.koreaherald.com/view.php?ud=20141229000898.

Kwon, Myungkwan. 2021. The accelerated growth OTT services due to COVID-19. *Donga Ilbo*, February 25. https://www.donga.com/news/It/article/all/20210225/105614577/1 [in Korean].

Lee, Hyunji. 2018. A "real" fantasy: Hybridity, Korean drama, and pop cosmopolitans. *Media, Culture & Society* 40 (3): 365–380.

Lee, Jeeheng. 2019. *BTS and ARMY culture*. Seoul: Communication Books [in Korean].

Lee, Min Joo. 2019. Desiring Asian masculinities through Hallyu tourism. In *The rise of K-dramas: Essays on Korean television and its global consumption*, ed. Jae Yoon Park and Ann-Gee Lee, 26–46. Jefferson: McFarland & Company, Inc.

Lee, Sangjoon. 2015. From diaspora TV to social media: Korean TV dramas in America. In *Hallyu 2.0: The Korean Wave in the age of social media*, ed. Sangjoon Lee and Markus Nornes, 172–194. Ann Arbor: University of Michigan Press.

Li, Yao, and Harvey L. Nicholson Jr. 2021. When "model minorities" become "yellow peril"—Othering and the racialization of Asian Americans in the COVID-19 pandemic. *Sociology Compass* 15 (2). https://doi.org/10.1111/soc4.12849.

Leung, Lisa Y.M.. 2021. Mediating Asian modernities: The lessons of Korean dramas. In *The soft power of the Korean Wave: Parasite, BTS and drama*, ed. Youna Kim, 184–195. London: Routledge.

Lundby, Knut. 2008. Introduction: Digital storytelling, mediatized stories. In *Digital storytelling, mediatized stories: Self-representations in new media*, ed. Knut Lundby, 1–17. New York: Peter Lang.

Lyman, Stanford M. 2000. The "yellow peril" mystique: Origins and vicissitudes of a racist discourse. *International Journal of Politics, Culture, and Society* 13 (4): 683–747.

Madianou, Mirca, and Daniel Miller. 2013. Polymedia: Towards a new theory of digital media in interpersonal communication. *International Journal of Cultural Studies* 16 (2): 169–187.

Middletone, Richard. 2020. MBC's South Korean format 'The Masked Singer' reaches 50 country milestone. *Television Business International*, January 13. https://tbivision.com/2020/01/13/mbcs-south-korean-format-the-mas ked-singer-reaches-50-country-milestone/.

Noh, Heeyoun. 2020. *KISDI (Korea Information Society Development Institute) STAT Report* 20 (4): 2–19 [in Korean].

Oh, David C. 2015. *Second-generation Korean Americans and transnational media: Diasporic identifications*. Lanham: Lexington Books.

Oh, Youjeong. 2018. *Pop city: Korean popular culture and the selling of place*. Ithaca: Cornell University Press.

Park, Jung-Sun. 2013. Negotiating identity and power in transnational cultural consumption: Korean American youths and the Korean Wave. In *The Korean Wave: Korean media go global*, ed. Youna Kim, 120–134. London: Routledge.

Park, Sojeong, and Seok-Kyeong Hong. 2021. Performing whiteness: Skin beauty as somatechnics in South Korean stardom and celebrity. *Celebrity Studies* 12 (2): 299–313.

Q on CBC. 2018. You don't have to explain yourself': Steven Yeun on the freedom of filming Lee Chang-dong's Burning in Korea. *CBC Radio*, November 1. https://www.cbc.ca/radio/q/thursday-november-1-2018-ren% C3%A9e-fleming-steven-yeun-and-more-1.4885983/you-don-t-have-to-exp lain-yourself-steven-yeun-on-the-freedom-of-filming-lee-chang-dong-s-bur ning-in-korea-1.4886013.

Seo, Min-Soo. 2012. Lessons from K-pop's global success. *SERI Quarterly* 5 (3): 60–66.

Soh, Leo. 2017. Our campus: Daniel Kim is saying goodbye to pop danthology. *The UBYSSEY*. February 1. https://www.ubyssey.ca/features/our-campus-daniel-kim.

Song, Hojin. 2018. The making of microcelebrity: AfreecaTV and the younger generation in neoliberal South Korea. *Social Media+ Society* 4 (4). https://doi.org/10.1177/2056305118814906.

Spangler, Todd. 2018. Warner Bros.' DramaFever Korean-drama streaming service is shutting down. *Variety*, October 16. https://variety.com/2018/digital/news/dramafever-k-drama-shutting-down-warner-bros-1202982001.

Wang, Claire. 2021. Jean Yoon of "Kim's convenience" on behind-the-scenes struggles with racism, representation. *NBC News*, July 20. https://www.nbcnews.com/news/asian-america/jean-yoon-kims-conven ience-scenes-struggles-racism-representation-rcna1461.

Wang, Runjie. 2019. "The Masked Singer" is a game changer in global TV. *PaleyMatters*, June 27. https://paleymatters.org/https-paleymatters-org-the-masked-singer-dc41a4364000.

Westerman, Ashley. 2019. "Kim's convenience" is a sitcom about Asian immigrants–with depth. *NPR*, January 9. https://www.npr.org/2019/01/09/682888290/kim-s-convenience-is-a-sitcom-about-asian-immigrants-with-depth.

Yoon, Kyong. 2020. Diasporic Korean audiences of Hallyu in Vancouver, Canada. *Korea Journal* 60 (1): 152–178.

Yu, Sherry, S. 2018. *Diasporic media beyond the diaspora: Korean media in Vancouver and Los Angeles*. Vancouver: UBC Press.

CHAPTER 4

K-pop Diaspora

Abstract For young Korean Canadians, K-pop (Korean idol pop music) is presented not only as an ethnic media form but also as a highly global media practice. The diasporic youth's consumption of K-pop may partly fulfill their cultural nostalgia and contribute to enhancing their ethnic ties with their ancestral homeland. Moreover, they appreciate K-pop as a global sound that is considered to be youthful, kaleidoscopic, hybrid, and relatable. While feeling ethnic and cultural affinities with K-pop, the diasporic youth engage with this genre as a cultural resource for questioning the mainstream cultural frame that takes Whiteness as a norm for granted.

Keywords Hallyu (The Korean Wave) · Diasporic youth · K-pop · Diasporic music · Ethnic identification · Hybridization · Fandom · Idol · BTS

On an American TV talk show in 2019, Randall Park, the star of *Fresh Off the Boat* (ABC sitcom 2015–2020) shared his experience attending a BTS concert (*The Ellen Show* 2019). The Korean American actor, who was not a fan of the group but simply accompanying his BTS fan wife, was moved by 90,000 audience members of diverse backgrounds singing along with BTS in Korean at the Rose Ball stadium. Showing a picture of himself watching the concert in tears with excitement, he said, "As a kid,

© The Author(s) 2022   101
K. Yoon, *Diasporic Hallyu*, East Asian Popular Culture,
https://doi.org/10.1007/978-3-030-94964-8_4

I could never imagine something like that happening. I just, I cried. (...) I am not ashamed." Similar to Park, many diasporic Koreans have "come out" as K-pop fans after their encounter with the recent Korean Wave (or Hallyu). In Canada, University of Toronto professor Michelle Cho identified herself as a K-pop fan (especially a fan of BTS) without shame during an episode of the Canadian radio documentary show Tapestry (CBC Radio 2020). As a diasporic Korean who was born and raised in Chicago and now living in Toronto, Cho recalled her feelings growing up as a person of color who had to be keenly aware of her cultural difference, and thus, she welcomed the K-pop phenomenon: "Seeing Korean popular culture find mainstream success in North America, in an environment where there really aren't many examples of Asian representation in popular culture, is moving to me in ways that I didn't even expect."[1]

As illustrated by Park's and Cho's comments above, the recent global K-pop phenomenon was not previously imaginable for most of the young diasporic youth interviewed for this book (and certainly not for their parents). An increasing number of people seem to "come out" and identify themselves as K-pop fans. Some K-pop fans interviewed in the early phase of this research (2015) spoke about their discomfort with publicly identifying themselves as K-pop fans due to the somewhat negative, racialized stigma attached to the music. However, as the research interviews with Korean Canadian youth progressed, it became evident that K-pop is no longer a marginal cultural taste. Not unlike many other countries, Canada has witnessed the rapid rise of K-pop since the mid- and late 2010s. In particular, with BTS's smash hits during the pandemic period, Korean songs began to be played on Canadian national and local radio and TV. Arguably, K-pop has become an icon of global popular culture (Jin et al. 2021).

To further the previous chapters' discussions of diasporic young people's identity work in relation to Hallyu, this chapter specifically focuses on young Korean Canadians' engagement with K-pop. Despite the increasing studies of global K-pop, diasporic Korean audiences have

---

[1] Despite the increasing recognition, backlash against and stigmatization of K-pop and Hallyu still exist. As a simple example, the first reader comments on the Canadian Broadcasting Corporation (CBC) news article reporting this Tapestry episode on K-pop explicitly disapproved of K-pop. The reader wrote, "They've ruined the kids with this garbage, why are you promoting it" (Reader comments on CBC Radio 2020, retrieved as of August 18, 2021).

been rarely researched. Korean Canadian youth engage with K-pop from their own unique audience positions equipped with bilingual and bicultural literacy—in comparison with Korea-based audiences on the one hand and overseas audiences (of non-Korean backgrounds) on the other. The Korea-based audiences may have grown up with Korean music (K-pop as a genre in particular) as a default popular music due to its continued expansion of the national music industry. According to a recent survey, the most frequently listened to music among Koreans was Korean/domestic popular music (83.6%), which was followed by Western-English (12.4%) and Japanese (2.2%) popular music (Korea Creative Content Agency 2020).[2] In comparison, Canada-based audiences are exposed to both Canadian and American music. In response to the strong influence of American media, Canadian media is required by the national regulator to program Canadian content for at least 35% of a popular music broadcast (Canadian Radio-television and Telecommunications Commission 2002; Connolly and Iino 2017).

Because Korean Canadian youth grow up in Korean immigrant families and in Canadian public schooling, Korean Canadians may navigate between these two different national soundscapes—domestic music-dominated Korea and American music-dominated Canada. Furthermore, as discussed in the previous chapters, while growing up, young Canadians of Korean heritage become aware of their "second generation advantages," which allow them to have multiple cultural and identity options (Kasinitz et al. 2008), and these advantages can be extended to the young Korean Canadians' cultural consumption patterns. Arguably, they are neither fully in the position of Korea-based audiences nor fully in the mainstream position of White Anglo Canadian audiences, and thus, Korean Canadian youth may experience K-pop differently than both of these audiences. For diasporic youth who are equipped with bilingual and bicultural literacy and thus can navigate between Anglophone music and Korean music, K-pop is neither the mainstream music of their own locale of residence nor simply a foreign music genre. Among diasporic youth, K-pop may be signified as a *national/ethnic* (Korean) cultural genre on

---

[2] In the same survey, when answers for the two most frequently listened to music are combined, the preference for Korean popular music was even higher (95.3%), which was followed by Western-English (73.7%) and Japanese (6.5%) popular music (Korea Creative Content Agency 2020).

the one hand and re-signified as a *post-national/postmodern* cultural form on the other hand.

Diasporic Koreans (as well as diasporic Asians) may have played an important role in the growth of K-pop and its fandom in North American youth cultures (Park 2013; Yoon and Jin 2016). Given that bilingual Korean American and Korean Canadian youth may operate as early adopters and translators, further studies of young diasporic audiences are needed. This chapter begins by discussing the multiple meanings of K-pop before reviewing findings from previous studies on diasporic youth popular music consumption and the potential insights and limitations of these studies for understanding diasporic youth engagement with K-pop. Drawing on in-depth interviews with young Korean Canadians, this chapter examines how these diasporic youth engage with K-pop in the process of growing up and what meanings are generated from their diasporic consumption of K-pop. In particular, this chapter examines how K-pop is interpreted not only as an ethnic cultural text but also as a global cultural text. Moreover, it addresses how K-pop is appropriated by diasporic youth as a cultural resource for challenging the White-dominant cultural frame.

UNDERSTANDING K-POP

K-pop often refers to Korean popular music, but such definitions may be too expansive to accurately capture the recent phenomenon of global fan culture triggered by major Korean idol groups, such as BTS, Blackpink, and Exo, to name a few. In reality, K-pop as a genre (as categorized in global music markets, charts, and media) may refer to a set of Korean music comprised of particular components and conventions. To be succinct, K-pop signifies "the music and dance of Korean idol pop groups" (Fuhr 2017, p. 283). More specifically, Shin (2017, p. 118) refers to K-pop as "Korean idol pop" whose music style involves "dance pop and, to a lesser degree, R&B ballad, along with some elements of hip-hop and electronica." K-pop is also known for its enthusiastic fanbases, especially via social media. For example, due to global K-pop fan engagement, K-pop idol groups BTS and Exo have significantly outperformed on Twitter far more than any other artists including Justin Bieber and Taylor Swift (Blake 2018). K-pop especially appeals to post-millennial Generation Z, who are born in/after the mid-1990s (Kang 2018). K-pop is no longer a music trend emerging in Korea or Asia, as major K-pop groups' overseas fanbases are estimated to outnumber their domestic counterparts (Tizzard 2021).

In analyzing this global phenomenon of K-pop, there have been debates about what constitutes K-pop and what the K in K-pop means (Fuhr 2016; Lie 2012; Jin et al. 2021). K-pop is undeniably a *Korean* cultural genre that rapidly reaches to non-Korean audiences across the globe. The genre is comprised of music performed by (mostly) Korean artists and in (mostly) the Korean language, and the systematic training/production system is often referred to as the "in-house system" (Shin 2009; Shin and Kim 2013). While the genre refers to made-in-Korea pop music products, the uniqueness of this genre is its exceptional level of hybridity in content and style; the K-pop industries have extensively absorbed Western music styles and genres and have expanded exponentially for decades (Anderson 2016; Jung 2011; Shin 2009). Due to its global nature, which also incorporates a postmodern and hybrid coalescence of music, visuals, dance, and fashion (Fuhr, 2016), it can be argued that K-pop is no longer "owned" by Korean audiences but has evolved into a cultural text and industry designed for audiences of different geocultural contexts.[3] The global nature of K-pop is deeply articulated with the genre's integration into digital and social media environments. Among various media forms that constitute Hallyu, K-pop has attracted rapidly increasing media attention especially since Psy's megahit "Gangnam Style" (2012) and BTS's series of record-breaking successes in global music markets since the late 2010s. Compared to Korean dramas (known as K-drama) and Korean films, which led the early phase of the Korean Wave between the late 1990s and the 2000s, K-pop particularly benefits from the development of social media and its expanding

---

[3] K-pop is known for its extensive overseas fanbases. Moreover, the industries have increasingly recruited non-Korean talents, such as non-Korean idol members (e.g., Blackpink and Twice), and collaborated with international composers, choreographers, and marketers. Recently, the K-pop industries have experimented with different methods of dissemination. For example, a major K-pop entertainment company, JYP, trained and launched a girl group comprised of 9 Japanese members in 2020, aiming to utilize the K-pop industry's insider knowledge and system for primarily Japanese markets. Furthermore, an experimental K-pop band, EXP-edition, comprised of all non-Korean members was launched by small K-pop label IMMABB Entertainment in 2017. For this project, the four members moved from the United States (US) to Korea in 2016, yet the group did not receive favorable reviews or find success in the domestic market. There have been controversies about this all non-Korean K-pop band, and some K-pop fans criticized this group as an example of cultural appropriation (Tubiera 2020).

user bases. It may be hard to explain why and how K-pop rapidly pene-trated the global music markets without considering the role of YouTube, Twitter, and Facebook, as well as many other specialized and networked digital media platforms such as V-Live (the personal broadcast platform for Korean pop culture celebrities, launched by the Korean Internet portal Naver) (e.g., Jin 2016; Jin et al. 2021; Jung and Shim 2014). As a highly digitally-driven and transnational cultural genre, K-pop has redefined itself as music that engages with local, national, and post-national dimensions of popular culture.

Until the late 2010s, when BTS achieved undeniable success in the global market and received rave reviews by Western critics and media, the K-pop industries were often viewed with skepticism in Western music markets. Some Western critics reduced this new cultural genre to a set of factory-made, commercially-driven commodities even until the early or mid-2010s. For example, American music critic Seabrook (2012) called the K-pop industry a "factory system" and noted that major idol groups are "seen by some as being too robotic to make it in the West." However, several K-pop idol groups—BTS in particular—have moved beyond such pessimistic predictions and achieved remarkable success in Western markets along with critical acclamation. In BTS's early, formative period, the group explicitly questioned mainstream critics' categorizing of them as idols and as factory-manufactured pseudo-artists. In BTS's song "Idol," whose songwriters include BTS member RM, the lyrics are: "You can call me artist. You can call me idol. No matter what you call me. I don't care. I am proud of it" (Hong 2020).

By engaging with K-pop's national and ethnic origin sometimes and its hybrid and cosmopolitan styles other times, global audiences have diversified this cultural genre's meanings—as a simultaneously national *and* post-national/postmodern genre (Jung 2013). K-pop indicates its national origin in its name (the "K" in K-pop); yet, K-pop as a set of "strategically manufactured, culturally hybridized popular products" has satisfied "the complex desires of some global mass pop-consumers" (Jung 2013, p. 117). The recent rise of K-pop in global music markets, espe-cially among young people, vividly shows how a local form of music, which has gone through phases of "mimicry" and "catching up with the West," undergoes a phase of local and global hybridization and furthermore moves toward "cultural cosmopolitanism" (Howard 2013) or "the latest stage of postmodern consumer aesthetics" (Fuhr 2016). In particular, for overseas audiences, the music can be received as the foreign (because of its Korean attributes) and/or the familiar (because of its post-national, hybrid musical styles). This oscillation between (and combination of) the seemingly contrasted attributes of being foreign and familiar often synergistically appeals to overseas audiences and fans. The geocultural distance (i.e., being foreign) allows overseas fans to escape their local contexts and imagine a new world, while the musical proximity and hybridity (i.e., being familiar) might lower the barriers for overseas fans to engage in this "foreign" music (Yoon 2019). As examined in this chapter, Korean Canadians' reception of K-pop may reveal the diasporic dimensions of the K-pop phenomenon—the ways in which K-pop is signified with different meanings especially between the proximal and the distant (or foreign) or between the ethnic and the global.

DIASPORIC POPULAR MUSIC AND YOUTH CULTURE

Diasporic popular music flows and practices offer an interesting example to understand how diasporas encounter and engage in their cultural heritage, and in so doing, generate particular transnational meanings. Among other cultural texts, music is a powerful cultural resource that associates lived experiences with collective memories and identity (Baily and Collyer 2006). In migration and music studies, transnational migrants and their descendants are seen as bearers of tradition and/or facilitators of musical innovation (Baily and Collyer 2006). For example, migrant audiences and musicians can serve to maintain their cultural heritage and cultural texts in other cultural contexts (the "host" societies), while altering cultural texts of their ancestral homeland in conjunction with those of the "host" societies. In particular, with advanced digital media technologies, the innovative role of migrant music seems to be accelerated through the constant remix and hybridization of musical forms. As music transnationally flows, along with musicians and audiences, it re-engages with its roots and explores its routes.

Diasporic young people's consumption of (ancestral) homeland music has been examined from several different perspectives. Among them, two groups of studies seem particularly relevant for K-pop-driven diasporic youth culture. First, a group of studies focused on the ways in which music from the homeland is utilized by migrant youth to better understand and connect with the histories and struggles of their ancestors and parents. For example, Maghbouleh's (2010) study of Iranian American youth and their consumption of pop culture of pre-Revolutionary

Iran illustrated that homeland pop music can be "a key indicator of the intergenerational transmission of nostalgia" (p. 202). According to the study, for the children of immigrants, diasporic and ethnic language music offers a resource for their desire to recover a lost home. The study also reveals that diasporic music is a tool to bridge the generation gap and to "articulate the production of culture and national identity" (p. 213). Moreover, diasporic music can also provide emotional shelters or boundaries for immigrants and their children. Aydin's (2016) study of Turkish migrants in Berlin illustrated that diasporic music served to make boundaries for migrants and thus produced an "enclave in which to take shelter from the difficulties of the outer world," while keeping their connection with the homeland alive (p. 216). At a community level, diasporic Turks' consumption of Turkish music functioned to transmit cultural memories and heritage; moreover, musical innovation (e.g., non-traditional musical styles and elements) emerged, and in so doing, cultural memories were constantly reshaped (Aydin 2016).

A second group of studies explored the process of cultural hybridization through diasporic experiences. According to these studies, diasporic youth do not only access ancestral homeland music for understanding and engaging with histories or for seeking emotional refuge. Certain forms of diasporic popular music are highly hybridized and relocalized in the "host" society and thus contribute to the reimagining and reshaping of diasporic audiences' ethnic identities. For example, *desi* music among Indian-American youth in Western urban settings reveals how ethnic pop culture is both a "backward" looking (i.e., connected with the past and histories) and "forward" looking (i.e., connected with the here and now) resource for children of immigrants who grow up exposed to diverse Western cultural genres. *Desi* is a translocally-grown diasporic youth culture, which includes practices of remixing Punjabi folk music over Western dance music genres, such as hip-hop and house, and the genre combining of Hindi film music with similar dance beats (Diethrich 1999, p. 35). *Desi* music scenes emerged in Western urban contexts, including London and New York City, and became a subcultural or counter-hegemonic cultural trend among young people of South Asian heritage (Diethrich 1999; Maira 2002). Several studies of *desi* culture commonly point out that this cultural phenomenon serves to provide diasporic Asian youth in the West with connection to their ethnic origin and a new, multicultural sense of belonging (Alexander and Kim 2013; Diethrich 1999; Maira 2000, 2002).

The existing studies show that diasporic youth engage with popular music that originated in their ancestral homeland as a resource for understanding and imagining their ethno-racial *past* and roots on the one hand and as a resource for negotiating their contested *present* identity positions and thinking about their *future* on the other hand. That is, diasporic music can serve to fulfill cultural nostalgia for immigrants and their children, while "conjuring myths of authentic pasts" (Alexander and Kim, 2013 p. 359; see also Aydin 2016; Maghbouleh 2010); simultaneously, it can be more hybridized and mixed with Western music styles, while formulating new youth cultural styles such as *desi*. These studies show a spectrum between which diasporic youth explore and imagine their ethnic identity through popular music. Despite their contribution to understanding the ambivalent and complicated nature of diasporic youth identity and its articulation with popular culture, the studies draw on case studies during a pre- or early social media period and thus may not be directly applicable to the recent, social media-driven K-pop phenomenon. Moreover, the existing studies primarily addressed the ethnic cultural aspects of diasporic music in regional contexts (intra-regional contexts at most) rather than the extensive global circulations of an ethnic/national music.

In comparison with the diasporic music and youth culture addressed in the aforementioned studies, the K-pop phenomenon involves unprecedented widespread, global, fan practices far beyond an ethnic or diasporic youth demographic. The global circulation of K-pop among young people is far more dispersed than the examples of ethnic music flows addressed in the previous studies and not driven only by diasporic youth. As argued in this chapter, the diasporic Korean population constitutes an early adopter group in Hallyu, but they may no longer be a core consumer group (at least in terms of numbers) as non-Korean overseas fans seemingly outnumber those of Korean backgrounds in the recent overseas K-pop market (ARMY Census 2020; McLaren and Jin 2020).

As further discussed in the remainder of the chapter, K-pop is a problematic cultural genre as it simultaneously signifies (a) made-in-Korea music (the "K") on the one hand and (b) pop music ("pop") that conforms to global trends on the other hand, and in so doing, K-pop attempts to hide its own geocultural roots (Fuhr 2016). This tension (or synthesis) between the "K" (national/ethnic attributes) and "pop" (pursuit of Western genre music's global appeal) may contribute to expanding the music's markets. For diasporic youth of Korean ethnic background, who are relatively acquainted with both Korean culture and Western pop music, the "K" and "pop" components may still seem contradictory, yet they may see the synergetic dynamism between the components. K-pop's dilemma (or synergy) between the K and pop may resonate with young Korean Canadians' own experiences and negotiation with their own hyphenated (Korean-Canadian) identities.

ETHNIC SOUND OF K-POP

K-pop was introduced as made-in-Korea products in Canadian media, which means young Korean Canadians consume K-pop as an ethnic identifier and signifier, to some extent. The "K" in K-pop unavoidably has ethnic and national meanings for its overseas audiences, including diasporic Korean youth who associate the K with the cultural heritage of their ancestral homeland. Of course, such ethnic identification is not the only way of signifying K-pop among the young diasporic audience. Diasporic youth can still negotiate and navigate among different potential meanings associated with K-pop. This negotiation process can be compared with the diasporic youth's own identity negotiation between different "ethnic options," as was discussed in Chapter 2 (Oh 2015; Song 2003). While young Korean Canadians are familiar with Korean media through their family's media experiences, their ties with Korean media are different from those of the first generation Korean Canadians. By examining the *what* and *how* of the diasporic young people's engagement with K-pop, this section explores how K-pop is integrated into their transition to adulthood and contributes to furthering their ethnic identification.

Growing Up and "Coming Out" as Ethnic

As immigrants and their children have been able to access their homeland media and ethnic media through ethnic TV channels, satellite TV channels, and more recently, the Internet, diasporic consumption is not unique to Korean Canadians. First generation Korean immigrants in Canada also accessed Korean music and media during the pre-Hallyu (or nascent Hallyu) period (Yoon 2017). However, compared to older diasporic audiences' access to their homeland media, young Korean Canadians' engagement with K-pop reveals a new tendency in terms of the what and how of diasporic media consumption. The content and format of K-pop (i.e., the what of diasporic K-pop) are not necessarily nostalgic and the youth selectively and critically engage with the hybridity of this advanced pop cultural form. Their consumption processes (i.e., the how of diasporic K-pop) are deeply integrated into digital media infrastructures enabling their individualized and participatory engagement across media and platforms.

For diasporic Korean youth, the recent K-pop phenomenon, which overlaps with their transition to adulthood, is noteworthy in terms of the what and how of diasporic cultural flows. In terms of content to be consumed (i.e., the what of cultural consumption), the recent wave of Hallyu does not necessarily involve traditional or somewhat essentialized notions of ethnic culture. In comparison with the first generation immigrants, the diasporic Korean youth who were born in Canada or moved while young may not inherently seek ethnic or homeland media; they choose a particular ethnic media form (such as K-pop, as opposed to conventional, pre-Hallyu Korean media) among various available media genres, including American pop music and TV dramas. Indeed, the young Korean Canadians interviewed for this book, who grew up in Canada and used English as their main language, selectively and critically engage with Korean media (Yoon 2020). The diasporic young people's interest in Korean media is significantly aligned with the recent wave of K-pop, in which highly hybrid and globally targeted media forms become main features. Their favorite K-pop artists were globally recognized idols and not the locally recognized singers typically liked by first generation Korean immigrants.[4]

In terms of music consumption patterns (i.e., the how of cultural consumption), the young people engaged with individual viewing and listening through smart digital media, such as the iPhone, when they were growing up. In so doing, they easily navigated and omnivorously consumed across different media genres and across Korean, Canadian,

---

[4] There were a few exceptional cases where interviewees listened to relatively old Korean ballad music popular for their parents' generation. For example, 21-year-old Sasha, who immigrated at the age of 6, was a fan of Lee Sun-hee, a veteran Korean singer who was born in 1964 and has been active since the mid-1980s. Sasha explained how she found out about the singer: "Because my mom always had interest in music herself she actually even has a lot of the Korean CDs at home. (…) because of my mom's influence I got interested more into Korean music." Another reason why Sasha was interested in older Korean music was that some of the older songs were remade by K-pop idols she also liked. For example, Lee Sun-hee's songs have been sung and remade by several younger Korean singers.

and American media, among others. At the time of the interviews, the preferred devices for media consumption were smartphones and laptops for most of the interviewees. Moreover, they accessed K-pop, along with other pop music or other media content, through social media or streaming platforms, which allow them to engage in fragmented viewing and listening. That is, family-oriented ethnic media consumption in a living room during their childhood shifted to individualized, fragmented consumption. Digital media infrastructure also enables their participatory consumption through various activities such as commenting, uploading user-generated content, and networking with other audiences (Yoon 2020). Interestingly, some young people also accessed Korea-based digital media platforms to get updated quickly about their favorite K-pop idols. For example, 22-year-old Meghan was one of several interviewees who frequently accessed Korean digital media platforms that livestream K-pop idols' personal broadcast: "Now I don't watch much traditional media. I watch more from my V-app (V-Live app) which is direct communication between K-pop idols and viewers. So they stream live videos kind of like Afreeca TV [i.e., Korean live streaming platform] but for K-pop idols." Scarlet, a 20-year-old second generation student in Toronto, who often hangs out with Korean Canadian friends and enjoys K-pop and other Korean media, identified two social media platforms she used to share K-pop-related information among her K-pop friends: "They would send me links through Facebook and KakaoTalk. Those are the two main ones, and LINE, but not as much, because they are like 'LINE isn't Korean' so I'm like 'Okay...' (laughs)."

The young Korean Canadians' engagement with K-pop appeared to be deeply interwoven with their transition to adulthood and development of a sense of ethnic belonging. While some interviewees' interest in recent K-pop gradually grew from their earlier interest in a range of Korean media, others engaged with K-pop relatively recently after a period of interruption. That is, during their childhood and adolescence, some interviewees lost their interest in Korean media and/or were more intrigued by the non-Korean language (American) media enjoyed by many of their peers. "I used to listen to Korean music as a little boy. But as I got older I liked hip-hop. It's always the mainstream music here. That's why I distanced myself from K-pop all these years," stated 28-year-old second generation Ethan, who recently became interested in K-pop. During childhood and adolescence, the "mainstream" culture often discouraged the diasporic youth from exploring further their interest in the Korean media to which they had already been exposed through their parents and ethnic communities.

For some interviewees who had an interrupted period in their interest in Korean media, the recent K-pop phenomenon, which was often represented by global superstars such as BTS and Blackpink and their global fandom, was a significant trigger that (re)ignited their interest in Korean media. For them, the recent K-pop music and performance were largely different from Korean media during the pre- or early Hallyu era. According to these interviewees, K-pop was also no longer an ethnic musical form but hybrid pop music that consists of various musical styles and appealing visual components. Thus, K-pop seemed to gain symbolic currency among diasporic young people and even among non-diasporic (e.g., White) young people. K-pop was considered by the diasporic youth as a refreshing cultural genre that was sharply different from the Korean music that their parents listened to in the pre-Hallyu era.

As discussed in the previous chapters, the young Korean Canadians' growing up involves phases of ethnic identification. While some diasporic youth attempted to hide their ethnicity during childhood, they gradually made an effort for ethnic identification in late adolescence and early adulthood. In particular, for many interviewees, entrance to university appeared to have substantially changed their peer networks and understanding of their own ethnicity. Most of the interviewees recalled that their interaction with other Korean Canadians and Asian Canadians on the university campus helped them feel "OK" to be non-Whites. Those who entered large universities in Toronto and Vancouver began to identify themselves positively as Korean Canadians and people of color in alliance with their Asian peers. As discussed in earlier chapters, this process of "coming out" as ethnic in college (Maira 2002) has been observed in existing studies of young Koreans in North America and other ethnic minority youth as well (Danico 2004; Kibria 2002; D. Y. Kim 2014; Oh 2015).

While diasporic youth gradually challenge the pervasive pressure of assimilation and explore their ethnic options, through which ethnicity can be a resource rather than a stigma, the recent Western media attention to Hallyu further facilitated young Korean Canadians' ethnic identification. Notably, the interviewees' childhood and youth (the 2010s) overlap with the period during which Hallyu was introduced to North America and several K-pop artists, such as Psy, BTS, and Blackpink, attracted

Western media attention. 19-year-old Noah, who grew up in White-populated neighborhoods, was not substantially exposed to Korean media until his mid-teens. He was not particularly interested in the Korean TV programs that his parent sometimes watched until he was hooked by Psy's "Gangnam Style" and then became dedicated to other K-pop bands. He described himself prior to his introduction to the Hallyu phenomenon as being "Whitewashed." However, when he moved to Toronto for work after high school, he was introduced to Korean media and culture. Like Noah, for some young people in this book, the recent K-pop phenomenon contributed to their voluntary ethnic identification in their late adolescence or early adulthood. K-pop, a made-in-Korea product that is considered to be more trendy and youthful than previous Korean popular culture products, was incorporated into the process of their "coming out" as ethnic and questioning the existing White-dominant cultural frame.

Ethnic Identification Through Hallyu

At the time of the interviews, most of the interviewees positively evaluated the circulation of Korean media in Canada and globally—by associating it with their ethnic identity or ethnic pride. K-pop as Korean pop music was particularly appealing to some interviewees who desired strongly to identify with the national and ethnic origin of K-pop. The tendency of strong identification with the (ancestral) homeland and its culture was especially evident among the 1.5 generation who had embodied memories of Korea. Yet, there were a few second generation interviewees who also expressed their robust desires to learn more and thus identify with Korea. For these youth desiring to identify with Korea (whether 1.5 or second generation), this sense of belonging and affiliation offered by K-pop is even more important than the particular style or content of the music.

Some interviewees were relatively dedicated K-pop fans and others were not, though they still frequently listened to the music as a way of feeling a cultural connection to their (ancestral) homeland. For example, 21-year-old second generation Paige was not a particularly dedicated fan of K-pop, but she deeply identified with K-pop: "I don't think there's anything really special about K-pop but maybe the fact that it is Korean and I am Korean. I was like 'Oh, Wow, my country is pretty cool!" Like Paige, some young people in the study considered the recent K-pop phenomenon as an opportunity for them to feel enhanced ethnic pride and identification (regardless of their preference in music genres). For example, Stella, a 24-year-old second generation professional who had never been to Korea and thus stated that "Korea kind of feels like a foreign country," still had a strong sense of ethnic identification when she listened to K-pop: "If someone said this is Korean music, if someone point that out, and it is a good one, then I feel *jabusim* (pride) about it." She was not a fan or follower of particular K-pop groups, but still enjoyed Korean music and felt proud of it.

As addressed in the previous chapters, some Korean Canadian youth considered themselves as "cultural ambassadors" to promote K-pop and Hallyu. The pride was also reinforced through the young people's feeling of regaining connection with their (ancestral) homeland via Hallyu. Through her participation in the K-pop soundscape, Rebecca, a 21-year-old undergraduate student who immigrated at the age of 2 and thus had no memories of the homeland, felt imaginarily connected to Korea again. She described her journey of "back to Korean media" and virtually returning to Korea along with her recent critical awareness of the White-dominant culture.

> (When I grew up) A good chunk of my life I was still into Western music and I didn't really care about K-pop. But then what ultimately brought me back (to K-pop) is the fact that I was Whitewashed and I wanted to stick with English but then at some point I was just like, "Oh, I kind of miss Korean and using Korean!" I guess. K-pop helps because most of the lyrics are in Korean and you get to see Korean people.

As Rebecca notes, K-pop serves as a means of ethnic identification for Korean Canadian youth. The interviewees tended to acknowledge that recent Hallyu contributed to their positive Korean and Asian ethnic affirmation. 20-year-old Dale, who immigrated at Grade 1 and much later encountered K-pop, joined a K-pop dance team in Toronto in his late teens. He commented on the process of his ethnic identification that occurred in his mid- and late teens.

> I really started to miss the Korean culture. I missed Korean people, I missed, talking about stuff that was more related to Korea. So now personally I think I would like to categorize myself as a Korean rather than a Canadian.

However, diasporic young people's ethnic identification through Hallyu and K-pop does not mean they always associate this cultural genre with traditional and authentic aspects of Korean culture. Their desire for ethnic identification does not simply mean their pursuit of ethnic roots transmitted from their parents. The diasporic youth in this book were not "passive conduits for their parents' nostalgia" and instead adopted and appropriated diasporic cultural symbols in ways relevant to their own experiences (Maira 2002, p. 147). While the diasporic youth noticed traditional cultural norms in Hallyu media content (e.g., respect for elders in K-drama or Korean entertainment shows), K-pop was not often associated with traditional or authentic aspects of Korean culture. Rather, as 20-year-old second generation Scarlet noted, "with K-pop you can't define Korea because there are other aspects to Korean culture." Like Scarlet, some interviewees did not want K-pop to represent an essentialized mode of Korean culture.

In this regard, public attention to K-pop could bring the diasporic youth uncomfortable feelings owing to the stereotypical and homogenous association of K-pop and Korean Canadians. Some of the interviewees questioned the assumption that associated them with Korean popular culture regardless of their actual cultural tastes. For example, due to their peer's stereotyping, they were often assumed to be K-pop fans. 19-year-old K-pop fan Cody sometimes felt uncomfortable about some of his peers who assumed he was a natural-born K-pop fan with sufficient knowledge about K-pop and Korean media: "Only because I am Korean, some people are like 'Oh, you know BTS?'" That is, minority audiences' ethnic identification through the K in K-pop may be contradicted by mainstream audiences' othering of the K in K-pop. Whether or not they came out as K-pop fans among peers, the young Korean Canadians interviewed for this book enjoyed the extensive availability and global recognition of K-pop. The diasporic youth sometimes proudly identified with the K in K-pop, but they were also worried about the essentialization of Korean culture as a narrowly or stereotypically defined ethnic culture in the time of growing attention to Hallyu media.

GLOBAL SOUND OF K-POP

K-pop seems to allow diasporic youth to engage with "here" and "there" simultaneously. That is, while the music brings the feeling of "there" (Korea) identified by the language and the brand (the K), it involves cosmopolitan imagination through its highly hybrid and kaleidoscopic styles, applicable to "here" and "now." By engaging with K-pop, diasporic youth also create their own versions of this cultural genre as an ethnic, local, and global form. For them, K-pop does not simply reflect its ethnicity. While the interviewees acknowledged their pride as ethnic Koreans with regard to the K-pop phenomenon, the meanings of K-pop for them were not limited to ethnic identification. As K-pop is increasingly recognized as a global cultural genre for young people, its diasporic consumption may not only allow the diasporic youth to pursue an authentic ethnic identity or to feel inherited nostalgia for the ancestral homeland. At some point, diasporic youth may dissociate from the ethnic implications of the music but enjoy its kaleidoscopic universe—in this process, K-pop as music originating in their ancestral homeland may be de-ethnicized (Milikowski 2000) and re-signified as a global youth cultural form.

Kaleidoscopic and Relatable

K-pop has been gaining cultural currency among young Canadians and defining itself as a global youth cultural form. In more recent interviews conducted in 2021, the interviewees strongly agreed on the increasing attention to K-pop among their peers. Indeed, the megahit K-pop group BTS has become a major player in global music markets, as shown by the group's records on major music charts including the Billboard Hot 100 since the late 2010s (McClellan 2021; Yonhap News Agency 2021). In this regard, K-pop is no longer signified as mainly an ethnic or national music genre. At least for its global fans, the K in K-pop has increasingly come to mean a transcultural signifier that moves beyond the geocultural context of its origin country Korea (McLaren and Jin 2020).

The interviewees considered K-pop as a new breed of pop culture that is more advanced than (or comparable with) mainstream American music. 25-year-old Luke described K-pop as a "very modern and urban" genre that is "more fast paced [than American pop]." Moreover, K-pop is distinguished from American or Canadian counterparts as K-pop artists have various qualities that can perform across different genres and platforms. 16-year-old Kimberly praised K-pop artists: "they sing, but not only they sing but they also dance, and most of them can rap and they are also trained for entertainment. They are also in a group setting, and so they can be more popular." For many interviewees, K-pop was considered to be overall more entertaining than American pop music. According to 19-year-old Beth, "K-pop is really entertaining. It's better than American music for building up fantasies about what you could do. It's a source of immersive entertainment rather than an entertainment that you stand outside of."

In this manner, the young people immerse themselves in the universe of K-pop, which is highly entertaining but not fully detached from their daily contexts. This imaginary space created through participating in K-pop can be referred to as the universe of "kaleidoscopic pop," as defined by S. Y. Kim (2018). She argued that fans engage with K-pop as a kaleidoscopic universe, which hybridizes different forms of performance and music through the convergence of various media platforms. K-pop music videos are examples of the kaleidoscopic aspect of this genre, as they often present "a flamboyant mixing of classical and kitschy, old and new, foreign and local elements, precisely to be able to travel across cultural borders in the age of global media" (S. Y. Kim 2018, pp. 96–97).

For the young people in this book, K-pop was not only music but a highly performative and visual genre. The performance of K-pop appears to distinguish the genre from its Western counterparts. Rebecca, a 21-year-old K-pop fan and cover dancer, pointed out that K-pop as a dance genre is unique and advanced compared to Western mainstream music. In particular, she noted that K-pop choreography is highly recognized among non-Korean peer cover dancers.

> How Korea is stepping up in terms of dance and their choreography is capturing a lot of people's attention. I have talked to so many people and they're like, "Oh, actually I saw K-pop dance videos and they were so cool, blah, blah, blah." Also K-pop idols look very different from the people you would see on American TV. And some people prefer changes so K-pop is just something fresh to look at.

The pleasure offered by the kaleidoscopic universe of K-pop does not occur outside of the audience's reality, but is the pleasure of engagement through identification with the music and artists. Given that pleasure through popular culture often stems from identification (with stars and objects) and imagination (Fiske 1987), it is not surprising that the K-pop universe is perceived by its diasporic fans as a kaleidoscopic *and* relatable universe. K-pop's kaleidoscopic universe is highly relatable for the diasporic youth as there are similarities between the youth and idols, both of whom are similar ages and going through transition to adulthood. Moreover, the interviewees thought that the idols' styles, fashion, and makeup were more applicable to their everyday contexts, as noted by 20-year-old Dale.

> They [K-pop artists] follow a very popular trend. I usually look at their style of clothing and try to see what I can actually pull off with my visuals. So, basically K-pop idols wear clothing that people can actually follow, while American singers wear clothing just to catch people's eyes and stand out.

Partly due to K-pop idols' frequent social media presence and communication with their fans through various platforms, such as Twitter and V-Live, the young people felt much more intimate with K-pop idols compared with Western pop stars. The frequent social media engagement by some K-pop artists (e.g., BTS) seemed to present them as a mixture of superstars and micro-celebrities; while superstars use conventional broadcast and mainstream media yet maintain a certain distance from their anonymous audiences, micro-celebrities build intimate relationships with their fans by sharing mediated stories of their ordinary lives through social media (Abidin 2018).

Kaleidoscopic and relatable attraction of K-pop idols and the K-pop universe is facilitated by K-pop industries' transmedia storytelling. Idols perform not only on stage but appear through transmedia platforms—TV shows, films, radio, video games, and personal broadcasting.[5] As discussed in Chapter 3, idol group members often appear in TV shows or vlogs to reveal their everyday lives and their feelings behind the stage. Grace, a dedicated Hallyu fan in Vancouver, described one of her favorite K-pop groups Mamamoo.

> I follow Mamamoo. They're only four people, so, they act like very close friends. Two of them are even friends from junior high. So they are very

---

[5] K-pop industries have developed one-source, multiuse marketing methods, in which a form of content (e.g., idol groups and/or their songs) is deployed through various platforms and formats. For example, idols appear not only on stages but also on film, TV dramas, entertainment shows (as guests or hosts), radio shows (as DJs), and in numerous advertisements for big corporations, including Hyundai, Samsung, and LG. Through this marketing strategy, the Korean media industry has rapidly increased its domestic and overseas profits (Seo 2012).

close to each other. They do a lot of skinship,[6] and then, I got into
Mamamoo because I was watching their video. It's a video of them playing
around in the car. And even though it's unedited, they, always, can't stop
fooling around, and then, they always make jokes, and there's a section
where they make their own song. And they're really good at it too. So it
made me start liking them.

By being immersed in idols' transmedia storytelling, some interviewees identified strongly with idols' transnational journeys to transcend
their local boundaries, especially in relation to their own diasporic experiences. Indeed, some interviewees identified their own diasporic journeys
and experiences of growing up with the K-pop idols' efforts for global
stardom. Speaking about Blackpink, an idol group comprised of three
diasporic Asian women (two Koreans raised overseas and one Thai) and
one Korean woman, 16-year-old K-pop fan Kimberly implied how she as
a diasporic person might identify with the diasporic journey of the idol
members.

I feel like some people can relate to that group [Blackpink] a little bit
more just because they also come from all over the world. I feel like people
really like that global effect and they've come a long way and they've even
performed at Coachella [i.e., The Coachella Valley Music and Arts Festival
in the US, where Blackpink performed in 2019].

For Kimberly, K-pop is global in the sense that it engages with the global
journeys and efforts of idol members (both Korean and non-Korean
members) to reach out to global audiences. As Kimberly pointed out, idol
members' efforts and diverse backgrounds make K-pop more relatable. In
this manner, for young diasporic audiences, K-pop appears to represent
global sound, not because it creates a globally hegemonic music style but
rather it involves the young members' global journeys which may resonate
with the diasporic young people's life experiences.

The young people in the study did not necessarily reduce K-pop to
the narrowly defined idol system but instead appreciated the multifaceted

[6] Along with the rise of Hallyu overseas, many terminologies of Koreanized English
(known as Konglish), which are used by idols and Korean media, have been introduced
to English-speaking Hallyu fans. For example, skinship refers to intimate physical contact.
K-pop fans overseas have increasingly become familiar with Konglish expressions and thus
use them.

talents and global efforts of the young idols and could relate to them. The interviewees humanized, and felt connected with, the K-pop idols, and in so doing, appeared to challenge the mainstream media discourse that disapproves of the idols as copycat products manufactured through "factory"-like systems (Seabrook 2012). For the interviewees, K-pop artists are young people struggling with their own diasporic routes and challenging such top-down, disapproving discourses. Overall, for diasporic youth, K-pop is signified as diasporic, and thus global, sound. From their perspective, the global sound of K-pop reveals how young non-Western idols make an effort to go global through diasporic journeys and share their experiences with their fans who may also be on their own life journeys.

Countering Through the K

K-pop's global appeal shows how the genre has evolved by targeting global audiences and markets, as illustrated by its extensive hybrid textuality (e.g., genre blending and English mixing in lyrics) (Chun 2017; Jin and Ryoo 2014). However, K-pop's high level of hybridity may not necessarily erase the K in K-pop. Rather, K-pop serves as a resource to move beyond the top-down signification of Hallyu—either as a Korean national export (as promoted by the Korean government and industries) or a racialized, marginal commercial trend (as constructed by the Western mainstream media).

First, some Korean Canadians questioned the association of K-pop with Korean national pride as commonly shown in the discourse of Hallyu as soft power—that is, the country's power that entices, attracts, and influences overseas audiences (Nye and Kim 2013). As Fuhr (2016) pointed out, K-pop may be "a result of strategic planning and a fostering of the domestic entertainment sector by state-national bodies" on the one hand and "utilized by the government to increase the nation's cultural capital" on the other hand (p. 10). The signification of K-pop as a national export has been promoted by institutional gatekeepers, such as Korean news media, K-pop industries, and the Korean government, who have often defined this cultural genre as a major export of Korea. In response to the strong association of K-pop with Koreanness, some interviewees were concerned about the increasingly nationalistic signification of Hallyu in media and among Korean audiences. Speaking of Hallyu, Luke, a 25-year-old 1.5 generation Torontonian, suggested a dissociation of ethnic or national meanings from popular culture texts.

> I don't think there's anything to worry about, or to be proud about. It's just what it is. There's not much significance. I mean, we really shouldn't attach that much significance into it, as Korean media, Korean government, and the Korean academia do nowadays. Because I watch a British TV series, it's not like I'm fully into British culture and you know, it doesn't. I'm just trying to find out what I really like, and I just consume it. And if I'm bored I'll leave, and if I'm not, then fantastic, you know.

Luke and a few others were cautious (if not skeptical) about such associations between Hallyu and Korea's ethnic/national pride. Luke believes audiences choose among pop cultural content and move between different items, regardless of the geocultural origin of the items.

Second, for the young diasporic audiences, K-pop was more than an ethnic music genre due to its hybrid and alternative nature. The K in K-pop appeared not to be simply essentialized as an unchangeable cultural component of Korea but rather to be re-signified as a component that reorients pop music. For some interviewees, K-pop was an alternative to, or a refugee from, the mainstream soundscape. While K-pop was commonly considered by the interviewees as a hybrid music genre drawn from American music styles, it also signified an alternative to American pop music. When asked to define K-pop, 28-year-old Torontonian Ethan, like many other interviewees, emphasized the genre's hybridity: "K-pop is like a whole mix of everything. But it has its own weird, unique sound." For the interviewees, K-pop is similar with yet different from mainstream pop music. Criticizing the market dominance of American-oriented Anglo-Western pop music, several interviewees hoped that the difference of K-pop would contribute to expanding the Western-centric global soundscape. In this regard, it is noteworthy that the interviewees lamented racial barriers in American pop music, which marginalize K-pop. According to them, K-pop was signified as ethnic or marginal music in Western markets, not only because of its musical attributes but also because of Western music markets' systematic discrimination of Asians and Asian cultures as the other of the default Anglo-American music. The aforementioned Ethan pointed out the "large racial barriers" that hinder K-pop's further rise in North America: "the majority White-based entertainment is a barrier for K-pop. K-pop musicians, someone like Ailee (Korean American K-pop idol). Probably this has to do with her race." Despite the increasing dissemination of K-pop, the diasporic young people considered K-pop subject to racialization in Western mainstream media and markets. This awareness allows the diasporic audiences to think about the White-dominant cultural frame they have experienced.

Through these processes of engaging with K-pop not necessarily as ethnic/foreign music but as a global cultural text that may contribute to diversifying the mediascape, the diasporic youth see K-pop not simply as a national export but as hybrid music that may also reveal the limitations of the existing Western-centric mediascapes. By consuming K-pop as global sound, the diasporic youth may realize that their own cultural difference may not be necessarily disadvantageous but instead advantageous (the "second generation advantages" discussed in Chapter 2). This critical awareness may offer counter-hegemonic moments that allow the diasporic youth to explore multiple senses of belonging to here and there without sacrificing or silencing either of them. Furthermore, as evidenced by global fans' participation in campaigns for social justice, such as BTS fan engagement with the Black Lives Matter campaign, K-pop can be utilized as a cultural resource for social change (Benjamin 2020; Bruner 2020). In this process, diasporic youth who are equipped with bilingual and bicultural knowledge may make a meaningful contribution.

Between Hybridization and Westernization

The diasporic youth engage with K-pop as a highly hybridized cultural form with multiple and flexible significations, which also may challenge the White-dominant cultural frame and mediascape. However, some interviewees considered the increasing incorporation of English and Western elements in K-pop as a potentially undesirable or problematic type of hybridization as the tendency was interpreted as simple "Westernization" of K-pop (or K-pop's imitation of Western pop music). For global audiences, K-pop is perceived as a made-in-Korea item and highly hybridized cultural form (Jin 2016; Ryoo 2009). The young people in this book see K-pop as global sound especially through its hybrid aspects, which they distinguished from mere imitation of Western music styles. For example, the increasing adoption of the English language refrains and rap parts in K-pop songs was considered by several interviewees as a detrimental component in enjoying the music.

For Dale, a 20-year-old in Toronto, K-pop's introduction of English parts was not particularly appealing as they were not necessarily effectively incorporated into the Korean lyrics of the songs. Dale assumed that the frequent use of English refrains in many K-pop songs might be intended to "appeal to the rest of the world." However, he noted that frequent, and sometimes irrelevant, use of English could be interruptive.

> There are many times when they say something in English and I can't even understand what they're saying. That has a huge impact on the song itself. I like listening to the lyrics and if I can't understand the lyrics, then it just kinda turns me off.

As Dale suggested, for Korean Canadian fans who understand the Korean lyrics without translations, the "almost random" insertion of English phrases may restrict the pleasure of their listening experiences. This Korean Canadian response to hybridization of languages in K-pop songs may be different from other global fans of non-Korean backgrounds. The use of the English language has been considered as a characteristic of K-pop, which positively appeals to international fans (Fuhr 2016; Jin and Ryoo 2014). Fuhr (2016, p. 66) argued that English in K-pop serves to build "a linguistic gateway through which international fans can easily connect with the [K-pop] songs."

Since the interview with Dale in 2015, the incorporation of English in K-pop songs has become more frequent. Several major K-pop idol groups released fully English-written songs, some of which successfully penetrated global music markets. Blackpink's diasporic Korean members Jennie and Rosé have respectively released their English solo songs in 2018 and 2021, which were overall positively received by Korean and global fans. BTS released consecutively three English-written songs between 2020 and 2021, all of which were exceptionally well received by global audiences ("Dynamite," "Butter," and "Permission to Dance"). Compared to earlier English mixing in lyrics in K-pop songs, in which English was written and sung by Korean artists, the recent tendency of using English by major K-pop idols reveals a more professionalized process in which English-speaking lyricists, producers, and/or singers (foreign-educated K-pop idols) are involved. While the effective use of English language in K-pop is welcomed by fans, many overseas fans, including some of the interview participants in this book, appear to prefer Korean-written songs, as the language is an important component for the K-pop artists to express their feelings and deliver their message (Lee 2019). In this regard, K-pop and its global fandom have contributed to challenging the tyranny of English language music in global music markets. For example, BTS's overseas fans prefer to call the seven members by their Korean names (instead of English names) and make an effort to sing along with their Korean songs (Hong 2020).

In this manner, some interviewees seemed to make a distinction between hybridization and Westernization, although the division may often be ambiguous. That is, K-pop's hybrid styles that move beyond the replication of American pop music (Bhabha 1994) are considered K-pop's constructive and positive attributes, but its attempts to imitate the Western cultural codes and styles (such as the incorporation of English lyrics and Western appearances) were not necessarily welcome. For example, 28-year-old Ethan was skeptical about several recent K-pop groups' highly Westernized fashion and appearance.

> Korean shows and musicians now don't look Korean. They look like Koreans who try to get Western features. And I personally hate that. It's pretty much like saying that looking Korean isn't good looking enough. And so that's why you have to get these Caucasian features, you know what I mean? I think that's a travesty in the Korean culture (…)

As Ethan points out, if perceived as a mere imitation or knock-off of American pop, K-pop may no longer be an interesting global cultural item to diasporic youth. While diasporic audiences were supportive of the cutting-edge, however hybrid, cultural aspects of K-pop, they were critical of its imitative aspects. As shown by their understanding of the hybrid and Western cultural components, diasporic youth can be considered as a critical and selective fan audience group in the mediascape of Hallyu (Yoon 2020) as they have bilingual and bicultural frames of reference to evaluate K-pop in relation to the mainstream pop music they also listened to.

As discussed in this section, young Korean Canadians negotiate, and contribute to, the different meanings of K-pop—especially as an ethnic and/or global cultural item. The ambivalent (and potentially contradictory) significations of K-pop between the ethnic and the global reveal the ways in which K-pop is hybridized and thus generates multiple meanings, depending on the audiences of different cultural backgrounds. In this process of meaning-making, diasporic young people's cultural literacy seems to play an important role. Several K-pop dedicated interviewees defined themselves as relatively knowledgeable fans and in so doing distinguished themselves from the Koreaboo-type Western fans who fetishize the difference of K-pop.[7] The young Korean Canadians' "second generation advantages" (Kasinitz et al. 2008) allowed them to contribute to translating and introducing K-pop to the global mediascape. A few interviewees were relatively actively involved in production of paratexts, such as subtitles, while some others shared their knowledge with other K-pop fans of non-Korean background. Several study participants interviewed in 2021—during and after the megahits of BTS's songs in mainstream music charts—spoke about occasions that their classmates (of non-Korean background) approached them to ask about or talk about K-pop. As K-pop becomes a popular cultural form among some young people, diasporic Korean fans may gain increasing symbolic power in the scene of K-pop fandom in Canada. Symbolic power in a youth subculture, which has been referred to as "subcultural capital," refers to the knowledge of and ability to perform a particular subcultural style (Thornton 1996). Subcultural capital comprises "artefacts and knowledge which, within a specific subculture, are recognized as tasteful, 'hip' and sophisticated" (Jensen 2006, p. 263). Over the period of this book project (2015 to 2021), it seemed clearly that K-pop and Hallyu media had advanced their symbolic values among Canadian youth. With their subcultural capital, young Korean Canadian fans negotiate multiple meanings of K-pop as ethnic and global cultural forms.

CONCLUSION

K-pop has increasingly expanded its global audience bases. The young Korean Canadians interviewed for this book, whose adolescence overlaps with the period of extensive global circulation and rise of K-pop, engaged with this emerging music genre both as ethnic and as global sound. Despite media discourse attempts to essentialize the meaning of K-pop simply as pop music made in Korea, the meaning of this pop culture genre is more complicated as the national signifier of the "K"

---

[7] Koreaboo is slang negatively used by Hallyu fans. The term refers to non-Korean fans obsessed with Korean culture (often without sufficient cultural knowledge). See Chapter 2 for further discussion about the Koreaboo.

is articulated with the "pop" component that resonates with hybridizing or Westernizing forces.

By consuming K-pop as ethnic and global sound, Korean Canadian fans obtain positive feelings about who they are and critically re-examine the White-dominant culture they were immersed in. The recent rise of K-pop subculture may help diasporic Korean youth confidently speak about themselves and the music they like without self-monitoring and awareness of the White gaze. In the time of Hallyu, young Korean Canadians who used to hide their cultural taste for Korean popular culture owing to discriminatory public gazes and stereotyping voluntarily "come out" as K-pop fans. Furthermore, K-pop may allow diasporic young people to perform and explore cultural identities between here and there through experiencing the tensions and hybridity of different cultural forms and norms (Maira 2002). By engaging with, and negotiating, the ethnic and global meanings associated with K-pop through transmedia experiences, diasporic Korean youth seek ethnic identification and explore multiple senses of belonging.

As introduced at the beginning of this chapter, Korean American actor Randall Park was touched by his feeling of immersion in the K-pop universe in which people of various backgrounds were singing together in Korean in a large concert location in the US. Meanwhile, Michelle Cho, a Canada-based professor of Korean heritage and fan of BTS, felt positively about the emergence and recognition of K-pop because the phenomenon offers Korean diasporas in North America "a kind of different sense of confidence or understanding of what they can contribute to society as opposed to having to downplay or even hide aspects of Koreanness (…)" (CBC Radio 2020). These anecdotes show how K-pop as an ethnic and global genre is meaningfully integrated into diasporic Koreans' identity work and sense of belonging.

Diasporic youth find K-pop kaleidoscopic, playful, and relatable. The imaginary kaleidoscopic space does not simply serve to fulfill ethnic nostalgia or to reinforce consumable urban sound. The ethnic and global sound of K-pop may offer counter-hegemonic moments and resources with which diasporic youth can question Western-centric, commodifying, or nationalistic forces. As early adopters and cultural translators, Korean Canadian youth may play a role in the progress of this new youth cultural practice. Moreover, as critical audience members, diasporic Korean youth may be keenly aware of Korea-based fans' nationalistic celebration of

K-pop on the one hand and the Koreaboo-type Western fans' fetishization and essentialization of Korean culture on the other. Young Korean Canadians' role as a bicultural audience in K-pop's global soundscape reveals the diasporic dimensions of Hallyu. Equipped with bicultural and bilingual literacy, the diasporic youth question Western-centric and White-dominant cultural production and consumption, while challenging the essentialization of ethnic cultures.

REFERENCES

Abidin, Crystal. 2018. *Internet celebrity: Understanding fame online*. Bingley: Emerald.

Alexander, Claire, and Helen Kim. 2013. Dis/locating diaspora: South Asian youth cultures in Britain. In *Routledge handbook of the South Asian diaspora*, ed. Joya Chatterji and David Washbrook, 350–362. New York: Routledge.

Anderson, Crystal S. 2016. Hybrid Hallyu: The African American music tradition in K-pop. In *Global Asian American popular cultures*, ed. Shilpa Dave, LeiLani Nishime, and Tasha Oren, 290–303. New York: New York University Press.

ARMY Census. 2020. ARMY Census 2020 results. https://www.btsarmycensus.com

Aydin, Pinar Güran. 2016. Drawing a homeland on the staff: Music of Turkey in Berlin. In *Transglobal sounds: Music, youth and migration*, ed. João Sardinha and Ricardo Campos, 201–220. New York: Bloomsbury.

Baily, John, and Michael Collyer. 2006. Introduction: Music and migration. *Journal of Ethnic and Migration Studies* 32 (2): 167–182.

Benjamin, Jeff. 2020. BTS and Big Hit Entertainment donate $1 million to Black Lives Matter. *Variety*, June 6. https://variety.com/2020/music/news/bts-big-hit-1-million-black-lives-matter-donation-1234627049

Bhabha, Homi K. 1994. *The location of culture*. London: Routledge.

Blake, Emily 2018. The strength of K-pop fandom, by the numbers. *Forbes*, April 4. https://www.forbes.com/sites/emilyblake1/2018/04/04/k-pop-numbers/?sh=4e01391048ab

Bruner, Raisa. 2020. How K-pop fans actually work as a force for political activism in 2020. *Time*, July 25. https://time.com/5866955/k-pop-political

Canadian Radio-television and Telecommunications Commission. 2002. Canadian content requirements for music on Canadian radio. https://crtc.gc.ca/eng/cancon/r_cdn.htm

CBC Radio. 2020. Tapestry: How K-pop band BTS is helping fans a world away navigate identity and hardship. June 5. https://www.cbc.ca/radio/tapestry/healing-power-of-k-pop-pandemic-playtime-music-for-the-soul-1.5600104/how-k-pop-band-bts-is-helping-fans-a-world-away-navigate-identity-and-hardship-1.5600109

Chun, Elaine W. 2017. How to drop a name: Hybridity, purity, and the K-pop fan. *Language in Society* 46 (1): 57–76.

Connolly, Tristanne, and Tomoyuki Iino, eds. 2017. *Canadian music and American culture: Get away from me.* New York: Palgrave.

Danico, Mary Yu. 2004. *The 1.5 generation: Becoming Korean American in Hawaii.* Honolulu: University of Hawaii Press.

Diethrich, Gregory. 1999. Desi music vibes: The performance of Indian youth culture in Chicago. *Asian Music* 31 (1): 35–61.

Fiske, John. 1987. *Television culture.* London: Routledge.

Fuhr, Michael. 2016. *Globalization and popular music in South Korea: Sounding out K-pop.* London: Routledge.

Fuhr, Michael. 2017. K-Pop music and transnationalism. In *The Routledge handbook of Korean culture and society,* ed. Youna Kim, 283–296. London: Routledge.

Hong, Seok-Kyeong. 2020. *BTS: On the road.* Seoul: Across [in Korean].

Howard, Keith. 2013. The foundation of Hallyu: K-pop's coming of age. In *First World Congress for Hallyu Studies.* October 18–19, Korea University, Seoul. https://eprints.soas.ac.uk/15929.

Jensen, Sune Qvotrup. 2006. Rethinking subcultural capital. *Young* 14 (3): 257–276.

Jin, Dal Yong. 2016. *New Korean Wave: Transnational cultural power in the age of social media.* Champaign: University of Illinois Press.

Jin, Dal Yong, and Woongjae Ryoo. 2014. Critical interpretation of hybrid K-pop: The global-local paradigm of English mixing in lyrics. *Popular Music and Society* 37 (2): 113–131.

Jin, Dal Yong, Kyong Yoon, and Wonjung Min. 2021. *Transnational Hallyu: The globalization of Korean digital and popular culture.* Lanham: Rowman & Littlefield.

Jung, Sun. 2011. *Korean masculinities and transcultural consumption: Yonsama, Rain, Oldboy, K-pop idols.* Hong Kong: Hong Kong University Press.

Jung, Sun. 2013. K-pop beyond Asia: Performing trans-nationality, trans-sexuality, and trans-textuality. In *Asian popular culture in transition,* ed. John A. Lent and Lorna Fitzsimmons, 120–142. London: Routledge.

Jung, Sun, and Doobo Shim. 2014. Social distribution: K-pop fan practices in Indonesia and the "Gangnam Style" phenomenon. *International Journal of Cultural Studies* 17 (5): 485–501.

Kang, Hyun-kyung. 2018. K-pop strikes chord with US post-millennials. *The Korea Times*, June 25. http://www.koreatimes.co.kr/www/art/2018/06/682_251242.html.

Kasinitz, Philip, John H. Mollenkopf, Mary C. Waters, and Jennifer Holdaway. 2008. *Inheriting the city: The children of immigrants come of age.* New York: Russell Sage Foundation.

Kibria, Nazli. 2002. *Becoming Asian American: Second-generation Chinese and Korean American identities.* Baltimore: Johns Hopkins University Press.

Kim, Dae Young. 2014. Coping with racialization: Second-generation Korean-American responses to racial othering. In *Second-generation Korean experiences in the United States and Canada,* ed. Pyong Gap Min and Samuel Noh, 145–165. Lanham: Lexington Books.

Kim, Suk-Young. 2018. *K-pop live: Fans, idols, and multimedia performance.* Stanford: Stanford University Press.

Korea Creative Content Agency. 2020. *The 2020 survey on music users.* Naju: Korea Creative Content Agency [in Korean].

Lee, Jeeheng. 2019. *BTS and ARMY culture.* Seoul: Communication Books [in Korean].

Lie, John. 2012. What is the K in K-pop? South Korean popular music, the culture industry, and national identity. *Korea Observer* 43 (3): 339–363.

Maira, Sunaina. 2000. Henna and hip hop: The politics of cultural production and the work of cultural studies. *Journal of Asian American Studies* 3 (3): 329–369.

Maira, Sunaina. 2002. *Desis in the House: Indian American youth culture in New York City.* Philadelphia: Temple University Press.

Maghbouleh, Neda. 2010. 'Inherited nostalgia' among second-generation Iranian Americans: A case study at a Southern California University. *Journal of Intercultural Studies* 31 (2): 199–218.

McClellan, Jennifer. 2021. "You know we don't stop": BTS tops Billboard charts (again), breaks world records with "Butter", *USA Today*, June 1. https://www.usatoday.com/story/entertainment/music/2021/06/01/bts-butter-tops-billboard-breaks-bunch-world-records-again/7466496002

McLaren, Courtney, and Dal Yong Jin. 2020. "You can't help but love them": BTS, transcultural fandom, and affective identities. *Korea Journal* 60 (1): 100–127.

Milikowski, Marisca. 2000. Exploring a model of de-ethnicization: The case of Turkish television in the Netherlands. *European Journal of Communication* 15 (4): 443–468.

Nye, Joseph, and Youna Kim. 2013. Soft power and the Korean Wave. In *The Korean Wave: Korean media go global,* ed. Youna Kim, 31–42. London: Routledge.

Oh, David C. 2015. *Second-Generation Korean Americans and transnational media: Diasporic identifications*. Lanham: Lexington Books.

Park, Jung-Sun. 2013. Negotiating identity and power in transnational cultural consumption: Korean American youths and the Korean Wave. In *The Korean Wave: Korean media go global*, ed. Youna Kim, 120–134. London: Routledge.

Ryoo, Woongjae. 2009. Globalization, or the logic of cultural hybridization: The case of the Korean Wave. *Asian Journal of Communication* 19 (2): 137–151.

Seabrook, John. 2012. Factory girls: Cultural technology and the making of K-pop. *The New Yorker*, October 8. https://www.newyorker.com/magazine/2012/10/08/factory-girls-2

Seo, Min-Soo. 2012. Lessons from K-pop's global success. *SERI Quarterly* 5 (3): 60–66.

Shin, Hyunjoon. 2009. Have you ever seen the Rain? And who'll stop the Rain?: The globalizing project of Korean pop (K-pop). *Inter-Asia Cultural Studies* 10 (4): 507–523.

Shin, Hyunjoon. 2017. K-pop. In *the sound of subaltern cosmopolitanism? In The Routledge handbook of East Asian popular culture*, ed. Koichi Iwabuchi, Eva Tsai, and Chris Berry, 130–137. London: Routledge.

Shin, Solee I., and Lanu Kim. 2013. Organizing K-pop: Emergence and market making of large Korean entertainment houses, 1980–2010. *East Asia* 30 (4): 255–272.

Song, Miri. 2003. *Choosing ethnic identity*. Oxford: Polity.

The Ellen Show. 2019. Randall Park loves BTS and isn't ashamed of it. https://www.youtube.com/watch?v=wXizW7ahJjo

Thornton, Sarah. 1996. *Club cultures: Music, media, and subcultural capital*. Middletown: Wesleyan University Press.

Tizzard, David A. 2021. Who likes BTS? A survey of 400,000 fans around the world. *The Korea Times*, March 28. https://www.koreatimes.co.kr/www/nation/2021/05/782_306147.html

Tubiera, Alecsandra. 2020. Are non-Korean K-pop groups like Exp Edition, Kaachi and 5High cultural appropriation–or is 'K-pop is only for Koreans' racist? *South China Morning Post*, July 2020. https://www.scmp.com/magazines/style/celebrity/article/3123759/bill-gates-and-wife-melindas-modest-parenting-style

Yonhap News Agency. 2021. BTS replaces Billboard No. 1 with new song "Permission to Dance". *Yonhap News*, July 20. https://en.yna.co.kr/view/AEN20210719008500315.

Yoon, Kyong. 2017. Korean migrants' use of the internet in Canada. *Journal of International Migration and Integration* 18 (2): 547–562.

Yoon, Kyong. 2019. Transnational fandom in the making: K-pop fans in Vancouver. *International Communication Gazette* 81 (2): 176–192.

Yoon, Kyong. 2020. Diasporic Korean audiences of Hallyu in Vancouver. *Canada*. *Korea Journal* 60 (1): 152–178.

Yoon, Kyong, and Dal Yong Jin. 2016. The Korean Wave phenomenon in Asian diasporas in Canada. *Journal of Intercultural Studies* 37 (1): 69–83.

CHAPTER 5

Conclusion: Diasporizing Hallyu

Abstract While Hallyu media itself may not be inherently counter-hegemonic, the diasporic audiences' critical engagement with the Korean Wave may enhance transnational Korean media's potential to challenge the dominant mediascape. The diasporic dimensions of Hallyu contribute to questioning the hegemonic forces that intensify the nationalistic and/or Westernizing processes of this transnational cultural trend. In response to the recent rise of Hallyu, diasporic young Korean Canadians engage with this cultural wave and negotiate different identity positions, associated with here *and* there.

Keywords Hallyu (The Korean Wave) · Diasporic Hallyu · Diasporic youth · Audience · Soft power · De-Westernization · De-Nationalization

In the midst of K-pop band BTS's dominance on the Billboard Hot 100 charts in the summer of 2021,[1] British music producer and DJ Mat Zo tweeted (Adams 2021), "I'm convinced k-pop is still niche in the west. Seriously, how many k-pop fans do you know personally? Is it possible corporations are pushing so hard cause it's not working?" After continuing his disapproving comments on K-pop, he even analogized the

---

[1] As of August 2021, BTS's English-language song "Butter" was the longest running #1 song of the year on the Billboard Hot 100 chart. The group stayed at #1 for 10 consecutive weeks (9 weeks with "Butter" and 1 week with "Permission to Dance").

growth of K-pop fandom to child grooming: "K-pop doesn't hide the fact that it's manufactured by grooming children into cultural icons." This popular DJ appeared to deny the presence of K-pop in mainstream music markets even in the middle of the record-breaking popularity of a K-pop band and its global fandom. These derogatory tweets reveal that the Korean Wave (or Hallyu) may still be othered by some gatekeepers in the Western-centric mediascape.

This incident is indicative of the ways in which the cultural wave of Hallyu has sometimes been overlooked or stereotyped in the West. Some mainstream Western media and gatekeepers have reduced Hallyu to a commercially oriented fad in a niche market that is primarily popular among Asian or Korean diasporas without due recognition of the global audience bases of transnational Korean media. Indeed, in *The New Yorker* magazine's online discussion of K-pop, American music producer Jeff Rabhan argued, "In the US market, there are about two million Korean Americans, or people of Korean descent. Without question, BTS or large K-pop groups are going to be able to sell tickets in New York City and certainly sell out in Madison Square Garden and can do well probably in the top 10 Korean American markets in the US. But beyond that, they can't" (*The New Yorker* 2020). Rabhan's attribution of the success of K-pop solely to the existence of Korean American consumers astonished two K-pop export panelists involved the discussion (Crystal Anderson and Stephanie Choi) and elicited their ridicule. Not only was Rabhan's argument challenged by the K-pop experts in the discussion, but global K-pop fans also harshly criticized his ignorant, Western-centric analysis of K-pop. In fact, scholarly and media observations have revealed the global composition of Hallyu audience bases far beyond diasporic Korean audiences (ARMY Census 2020; Bruner 2020; McLaren and Jin 2020).

While this book has focused on diasporic Korean youth in Canada, it does not suggest that diasporic Koreans constitute the majority of global Hallyu audiences. Indeed, the book works to acknowledge the ways in which Hallyu is driven by fan audiences of diverse backgrounds. As revealed in the book, Hallyu emerges as a global media practice that should not be reduced to media that is consumed predominantly in ethnic communities overseas. Even the Korean Canadian youth in the study engaged with Hallyu not necessarily as ethnic media flows; for them, Hallyu was also signified as a kaleidoscopic and youthful universe.

Against this background, this book has examined the diasporic dimensions of the Korean Wave. Drawing on qualitative interviews with 40 participants in three Canadian cities, it has explored how Korean Canadian youth negotiated their cultural identity through a new popular cultural trend that originated in their (ancestral) homeland but has been circulated globally. The analysis has shown the diasporic youth's identity work while growing up in between different cultural contexts and in between different media texts.

Many of the young people interviewed for this book had been immersed in (pre-Hallyu) Korean media through their upbringing in Korean immigrant families. While some interviewees continued to enjoy Korean media during their transition to adulthood, others lost their interest in Korean media during their adolescence and turned to mainstream Anglophone or other types of media. However, for most of the interviewees, the recent version of Korean media that emerged since the 2010s (often referred to as the period of Hallyu 2.0, or the New Korean Wave) seemed to trigger (or re-ignite) their excitement and interest in particular Korean media genres, such as K-pop, Korean dramas (known as K-drama), and Korean entertainment shows.

As illustrated in this book, recent Hallyu media gradually changed the young Korean Canadians' perception of Korean media from *ethnic* media that is consumed mainly in ethnic communities to maintain their connection with the left-behind homeland to *global* media that introduces a kaleidoscopic and youthful universe. In particular, for the diasporic youth, K-pop was often considered a genre (among other Hallyu media genres) that contributed the most to redefining Hallyu not as the overseas circulation of ethnic or heritage media, but rather as a new kind of global youth practice through which young people simultaneously negotiate here (Canada) and there (Korea).

On the one hand, the book has shown that Hallyu media can be considered to be *ethnic* media as it allows the diasporic youth to vividly imagine the (ancestral) homeland that otherwise would have remained distant. Through enhanced association with their Korean cultural heritage and through pop cultural artifacts and imaginations, Korean Canadian youth explore "ties with the 'homeland' to find a symbolic or literal 'home' where they can sense what it is like to be, for once, part of the racial majority" (N. Y. Kim 2018, p. 294). One the other hand, the book has revealed that Hallyu media represents a *global* media form, comprised of kaleidoscopic, youthful, alternative, and hybrid cultural texts for an increasing number of overseas fan audiences including diasporic Korean youth.

As examined in this book, young Korean Canadians equipped with bilingual and bicultural literacy navigate different media forms through digital platforms. They not only navigate between different media (e.g., Western Anglophone and Korean media) but also assume different audience positions as early adopters, mundane consumers, and/or dedicated fans. The diasporic media experiences show that Hallyu is an evolving cultural process through which different meanings of transnational media are generated and negotiated from the perspectives of the audience who navigate different frames of reference here *and* there. To move beyond a Western-centric or a nation-statist perspective, this book proposes further exploration of the diasporic dimensions of the Korean Wave.

DE-WESTERNIZING AND DE-NATIONALIZING HALLYU

Diasporic cultural flows imply "how home is not a stable category" (Kalra et al. 2005, p. 18). Home may no longer remain a place of residence or nationality but may be redefined as places of imagination and affiliation. By imagining here through there, or there through here, in the time of Hallyu, young Korean Canadians may question where they are and who they are. While being *here*, diasporic youth are increasingly exposed to more relatable, non-White stars and texts and realize how the White-dominant cultural frame persists in "multicultural" Canada. In this frame, Hallyu is underestimated and racialized at best. Simultaneously, while being *there*, the diasporic youth also challenge the discourse that reduces Hallyu to the achievement of national "soft power."

De-Westernizing Hallyu While Here

As a non-Western popular cultural trend, Hallyu may offer Korean and Asian diasporas the leverage to reveal the dominant cultural norm that hides the existing discrimination and injustice against people of color and thus to problematize the taken-for-granted mediascape of seemingly multicultural Canada. Hallyu media can be a litmus paper with which the limitations of the White, Western-centric mediascape are tested. The increasing appearance and discourses of K-pop idols on social media and even mainstream media in Canada remind us that the mainstream media available in Canada might be in fact merely a segment of possible imaginations and thus represents a hegemonic world view instead of many other possible views. In this regard, the emergence of Hallyu may serve to do what Chakrabarty (1992) refers to as "provincializing the West," which is a process of dismantling the colonial hierarchy between the Western center and the rest. In this way, the West as the default and universal norm can be challenged. In a similar vein, J. O. Kim (2021) has recently proposed using K-pop as a "method" to facilitate various modes of transcultural meaning making and to explore alternative possibilities to question and subvert Western-oriented norms and cultural flows (J. O. Kim 2021).

Indeed, some young people interviewed for this book appeared to engage with the Hallyu media while learning to question the White-dominant cultural frame. They become critically aware of taken-for-granted White-dominant representations (and lack of Asian representations) in the Canadian mediascape. By watching BTS's performances on network TV or K-dramas available on Netflix, some interviewees now realized that there had been no Korean (or even Asian) TV characters in Canadian media. As the interview participants commonly noted, the default characters in media content were always White and thus they did not have room for even thinking about the absence or stereotyping of racialized people. By increasingly engaging with non-Western media forms in Western contexts, diasporic youth are reminded that Canada is a nation-state established through settler colonialism and diasporic routes of settlers of different kinds; and the White, Western lens may be an ignorant, violent, or partial (at best) way of representing worlds and identities. Hallyu has opened a new door for the diversified modes of the global mediascape in which the dominance of Anglophone Western cultural content and representations are questioned. Hallyu exposes the diasporic audiences to non-White stars and non-English languages, with which they can identify and thus eventually imagine "here" as not a White-dominant space, but deeply connected with "there" as a place that would have remained abstract and distant without the moments of engagement often occurring through mediation (i.e., the ancestral homeland, which would have remained purely nostalgic *without* the recent wave of Hallyu). Members of BTS and Bong Joon-ho, the director of *Parasite,* often speak in Korean in their interviews and speeches in Western media and thus require translations and translators. Hallyu may remind global audiences of the simple fact that English (or any other dominant language) is not a default language-setting in international cultural exchanges and consumption, but *translation is a default protocol* in transnational media flows and transcultural encounters. In an interview with an American magazine about *Parasite*, the director Bong described the American Academy Awards, known as The Oscars, as a "very local" film festival (Jung 2019). This account reminds Western audiences (and global audiences) that The Oscars is not a global event at all despite global media attention to it. Director Bong's account may reveal a potential way of provincializing (rather than conforming to) the West.

De-Nationalizing Hallyu While There

By enhancing their ethnic identification in late adolescence or later ("coming out" as ethnic in college), diasporic youth tend to explore their ethnic identities. The recent Hallyu media play a role in this transitional journey, as it contributes to the diasporic youth's feelings of connection with their ethnic heritage and senses of belonging. However, as some interviewees noted, the nation-statist definition of Hallyu as only a set of Korean media exports restricts the Wave's diasporic meanings. The celebratory, top-down discourse of the Korean Wave as soft power and national brand is seen as problematic by young people of diaspora, who do not belong to Korea as a nation-state. Several interviewees in this book were critical about the ways in which Hallyu is shaped from above by institutional power—such as the Korean government, industries, and Western media. As evidenced by the flourishing discourse of Hallyu as soft power, this cultural trend has been utilized to instrumentalize the "national" cultural form for maximizing economic or political gains (H.-K. Lee 2018). It is undeniable that the Korean government has heavily promoted the Korean Wave as a way of boosting its economy and as an ideological means to affirm national pride and cultural nationalism. Consecutive governments, regardless of their political stances, have continued their emphasis on Korean Wave-related campaigns, investments, and policies through "K-branding" (Kim and Jin 2016).[2] These efforts clearly

[2] The Korean government and cultural industries have made an explicit effort to take advantage of the K component (Bang 2020). Not only K-pop and K-drama but also other "K"-products (such as K-cosmetics and K-tourism packages) have been promoted extensively. K-products and brands are often combined to maximize their synergetic effects. For example, K-pop idols appear to endorse K-cosmetic products; K-pop tours in Gangnam (where some K-pop companies and merchandise shops are located) are a popular K-tourism package. The government has extensively used the K prefix to proudly refer to economic or policy sectors that might be relatively advanced in a global scale. As a recent example, the government celebrated its somewhat effective disease control system in the

illustrate Korea's desire to catch up, compete, and stand out in global cultural markets. The government-led, top-down discourses of Hallyu for the past two decades reveal the country's desire to be a global dominant or "standard" through export-oriented economic strategies which have been pursued especially since the 1990s (T. Y. Kim 2021; Kim and Jin 2016). The top-down discourse of Hallyu has emphasized the potential economic or political power to be gained through the exportation of transnational Korean media and cultural products. The "soft power" or "cultural diplomacy" discourse around the Hallyu phenomenon reveals nationalistic desires for maximizing the country's influence in the world. If Hallyu is defined as outbound flows and global market expansion of Korean media and culture, this phenomenon may be none other than the mirroring of the existing Western cultural hegemony.

In response to this nation-statist discourse of Hallyu, diasporic youth's engagement with transnational Korean media—an engagement that sometimes questions the essentialized mode of Koreanness from their bicultural audience position of being here and there, or being (legally and physically) in Canada and (ethno-culturally) in Korea—reveals that Hallyu cannot be simply defined by the institutional, top-down discourse in which Korean culture is instrumentally used, measured, and commodified for economic and political gains. From below, Hallyu involves multi-faceted audience practices in which diverse audience members generate different meanings in relation to their everyday contexts while refusing to reduce the cultural flow to a national product.

For diasporic youth, Hallyu may provide the possibility for different identities and cultures to be appreciated and hybridized without necessarily being subject to, but rather in negotiation with, the dominant Western, White gaze and the nation-statist discourse of Hallyu that reinforces (long-distance) nationalism. This new cultural trend seems to offer the diasporic youth an antidote to both the essentialized notion of Koreanness and the White-dominant imagination of Canada. The diasporic

---

early months of the COVID-19 pandemic in 2020 by referring to it as "*K-bangyeok*" (K-quarantine) (Yoon 2021). The extensive K-branding reveals the ways in which nationalism or national pride is commodified or politically utilized. Critics and young people have increasingly been fatigued by the extensive and self-celebratory tone of K-branding. Thus, K-branding is also disapprovingly considered as an example of "*gukbbong*" ("intoxication with nationalism"; *guk* means country and *bbong* means a slang for methamphetamine) (T. Y. Kim 2021).

engagement with Hallyu can contribute to provincializing both the West and the nation-state.

Hallyu as Diasporic Cultural Practice

The dynamic ebbs and flows of the wave show how media is diasporically circulated beyond nation-statist and/or Western-oriented mediascapes, and in so doing may allow diasporic youth to feel at home in different locations, moving beyond the binary opposition between here and there in their cultural practices. The transnational cultural flows of Hallyu can potentially generate new identities that are neither clearly affiliated with the nation-state form (Kalra et al. 2005) nor subject to the White gaze. Thus, young Korean Canadians' critical engagement with Hallyu media may offer opportunities for alternative cultural moments. The diasporic analysis of Hallyu allows for the possibility of provincializing the West, while rethinking the celebratory discourse about Hallyu as nation-statist soft power. The wave of transnational Korean media and popular culture may suggest that the global mediascape is increasingly diasporic in its meaning-making processes, which consequently allow it to move beyond the boundaries of nation-states.

Before concluding this book, it should be emphasized that Hallyu is not inherently counter-hegemonic against the Western-centric or nation-statist forces. In fact, mainstream Hallyu media has not been free of criticism due to its commercial interests. For example, K-pop industries have been criticized for their harsh training and control of idol groups to maximize profits (G. Kim 2018). Indeed, K-pop entertainment companies skillfully exploit fan participation to penetrate the market and generate profit, using "free labor" in the form of voluntary fan activities to generate profits without any substantial rewards (Y. Kim 2015; Proctor 2021). Moreover, it has been observed that the Hallyu industry has extensively developed somatechnics to fantasize about Whiteness especially through the obsessive emphasis on the white skins of celebrities (Park and Hong 2021). These examples contribute to the debates about the counter-hegemonic potential of Hallyu as a non-Western-centric cultural trend. No different from any other major media industries, the Hallyu industries seek to maximize profits through the instrumental use of culture as a commodity. Hallyu is certainly not free of the enormous structural forces of commodification.

However, the structural forces do not necessarily determine how Hallyu evolves as a transnational process that involves various stakeholders. In particular, as audience studies have explored, transnational media is constantly negotiated and relocalized through different modes of audience engagement (Athique 2017). Encountering the ebbs and flows of Hallyu media, audiences of different identity positions re-create the meanings of Hallyu media that would otherwise have remained an essentialized, foreign commodity form. In this transnational process of audience engagement, diasporic Korean youth play a unique role. As discussed in this book, young Korean Canadians engage with Hallyu media in relation to their own identity work that occurs in between cultures. Without necessarily relying on the Western-centric and/or nation-statist frames of reference, the diasporic youth may explore their audience positions transnationally and transculturally—between here and there. In so doing, they may also challenge the structural forces that attempt to define Hallyu as an essentialized commodity form.

As revealed by the examples provided throughout the book, young Korean Canadians may not assume a homogenous audience position. Some diasporic youth exhibited a stronger emotional attachment with the K, especially as an imagined refuge from the White-dominant cultural frame that has oppressively racialized them. In comparison, other diasporic youth reflected their second generation advantages or bicultural literacy as a means of negotiating the commodifying forces implicated in Hallyu. Moreover, there are groups of 1.5 and second generation Korean youth who are indifferent to, or even in denial of, Hallyu—especially those who are called "bananas" or the "Whitewashed." Different diasporic experiences and positions imply that the diasporic dimensions of Hallyu are multifaceted and open to further research. For example, various intersectional experiences of diasporic youth, which have not been fully explored in this book, require additional in-depth studies.

Among various audience groups, diasporic youth who take up relatively ambivalent reception positions between two (or more) national and cultural contexts reflect the ways in which Hallyu is appropriated in different contexts and generate both ethnic or national cultural flows and global cultural flows. By examining the Korean Wave as diasporic cultural practices rather than the diffusion of national cultural products and capital, this book has revealed the diversified ways in which cultural flows are negotiated, re-signified, and reappropriated by audiences who are in between here and there. Questioning the dominant global mediscape, diasporic Hallyu offers a new lens for understanding diaspora, media, and identity.

REFERENCES

Adams, Skylar. 2021. British DJ Mat Zo criticizes K-pop's "Child grooming" ways, while crediting corporations for BTS's success. https://www.koreaboo.com/news/dj-mat-zo-criticize-kpop-child-grooming-corporation-bts.

ARMY Census. 2020. ARMY Census 2020 results. https://www.btsarmycensus.com.

Athique, Adrian. 2017. *Transnational audiences: Media reception on a global scale*. Cambridge: Polity.

Bang, Joon-ho. 2020. The revival of the government's "K-promotion" brand strategy. *Hankyoreh*, January.12. https://english.hani.co.kr/arti/english_edition/e_national/924091.html.

Bruner, Raisa. 2020. How K-pop fans actually work as a force for political activism in 2020. *Time*, July 25. https://time.com/5866955/k-pop-political.

Chakrabarty, Dipesh. 1992. Provincializing Europe: Postcoloniality and the critique of history. *Cultural Studies* 6 (3): 337–357.

Jung, E. Alex. 2019. Bong Joon-ho's dystopia is already here. *Vulture*, October 7. https://www.vulture.com/209/10/bong-joonho-parasite.html.

Kalra, Virinder, Raminder Kaur, and John Hutnyk. 2005. *Diaspora and hybridity*. London: Sage.

Kim, Ju Oak. 2021. BTS as method: A counter-hegemonic culture in the network society. *Media, Culture & Society* 43 (6): 1061–1077.

Kim, Gooyong. 2018. *From factory girls to K-pop idol girls: Cultural politics of developmentalism, patriarchy, and neoliberalism in South Korea's popular music industry*. Lanham: Lexington.

Kim, Nadia Y. 2018. Race-ing the Korean American experience. In *A companion to Korean American studies*, ed. Rchael Miyung Joo and Shelley Sang-Hee Lee, 267–303. Leiden: Brill.

Kim, Yeran. 2015. Globalization of the privatized self-image: The reaction video and its attention economy on YouTube. In *Routledge handbook of new media in Asia*, ed. Larissa Hjorth and Olivia Khoo, 345–354. Routledge.

Kim, Tae Young. 2021. The state's roles in the development of cultural industries: Korean cultural industry policies from 1993 and 2021. PhD thesis. Simon Fraser University.

Kim, Taeyoung, and Dal Yong Jin. 2016. Cultural policy in the Korean Wave: An analysis of cultural diplomacy embedded in presidential speeches. *International Journal of Communication* 10: 5514–5534.

Lee, Hye-Kyung. 2018. *Cultural policy in South Korea: Making a new patron state*. London: Routledge.

McLaren, Courtney, and Dal Yong Jin. 2020. "You can't help but love them": BTS, transcultural fandom, and affective identities. *Korea Journal* 60 (1): 100–127.

Park, Sojeong, and Seok-Kyeong Hong. 2021. Performing Whiteness: Skin beauty as somatechnics in South Korean stardom and celebrity. *Celebrity Studies* 12 (2): 299–313.

Proctor, Jasmine. 2021. Labour of love: Fan labour, BTS, and South Korean soft power. *Asia Marketing Journal* 22 (4): 79–101.

The New Yorker. 2020. Experts explain how K-pop exploded in America. https://www.youtube.com/watch?v=ZCOGl9p08rg.

Yoon, Kyong. 2021. Digital dilemmas in the (post-) pandemic state: Surveillance and information rights in South Korea. *Journal of Digital Media & Policy* 12 (11): 67–80.

INDEX

© The Author(s), under exclusive license to Springer Nature Switzerland AG 2022
K. Yoon, *Diasporic Hallyu*, East Asian Popular Culture, https://doi.org/10.1007/978-3-030-94964-8

The manufacturer's authorised representative in the EU is Springer
Nature Customer Service Centre GmbH, Europaplatz 3, 69115 Heidelberg,
Germany. If you have any concerns regarding our products, please
contact ProductSafety@springernature.com

Printed and bound by CPI Group (UK) Ltd, Croydon, CR0 4YY

24/04/2026

02096345-0008